Carnegie Commission on Higher Education
Sponsored Research Studies

THE MULTICAMPUS UNIVERSITY:
A STUDY OF ACADEMIC GOVERNANCE
Eugene C. Lee and Frank M. Bowen

INSTITUTIONS IN TRANSITION:
A PROFILE OF CHANGE IN HIGHER
EDUCATION
Harold L. Hodgkinson

EFFICIENCY IN LIBERAL EDUCATION:
A STUDY OF COMPARATIVE INSTRUC-
TIONAL COSTS FOR DIFFERENT WAYS
OF ORGANIZING TEACHING-LEARNING
IN A LIBERAL ARTS COLLEGE
Howard R. Bowen and Gordon K. Douglass

A DEGREE AND WHAT ELSE:
CORRELATES AND CONSEQUENCES OF
A COLLEGE EDUCATION
*Stephen B. Withey, Jo Anne Coble, Gerald
Gurin, John P. Robinson, Burkhard Strumpel,
Elizabeth Keogh Taylor, and Arthur C. Wolfe*

CREDIT FOR COLLEGE:
PUBLIC POLICY FOR STUDENT LOANS
Robert W. Hartman

MODELS AND MAVERICKS:
A PROFILE OF PRIVATE LIBERAL
ARTS COLLEGES
Morris T. Keeton

BETWEEN TWO WORLDS:
A PROFILE OF NEGRO HIGHER
EDUCATION
Frank Bowles and Frank A. DeCosta

BREAKING THE ACCESS BARRIERS:
A PROFILE OF TWO-YEAR COLLEGES
Leland L. Medsker and Dale Tillery

ANY PERSON, ANY STUDY:
AN ESSAY ON HIGHER EDUCATION
IN THE UNITED STATES
Eric Ashby

THE NEW DEPRESSION IN HIGHER
EDUCATION:
A STUDY OF FINANCIAL CONDITIONS
AT 41 COLLEGES AND UNIVERSITIES
Earl F. Cheit

FINANCING MEDICAL EDUCATION:
AN ANALYSIS OF ALTERNATIVE
POLICIES AND MECHANISMS
Rashi Fein and Gerald I. Weber

HIGHER EDUCATION IN NINE
COUNTRIES:
A COMPARATIVE STUDY OF COLLEGES
AND UNIVERSITIES ABROAD
*Barbara B. Burn, Philip G. Altbach, Clark
Kerr, and James A. Perkins*

BRIDGES TO UNDERSTANDING:
INTERNATIONAL PROGRAMS OF AMER-
ICAN COLLEGES AND UNIVERSITIES
Irwin T. Sanders and Jennifer C. Ward

GRADUATE AND PROFESSIONAL EDU-
CATION, 1980:
A SURVEY OF INSTITUTIONAL PLANS
Lewis B. Mayhew

75363

i

THE AMERICAN COLLEGE AND AMERI-CAN CULTURE:
SOCIALIZATION AS A FUNCTION OF HIGHER EDUCATION
Oscar and Mary F. Handlin

RECENT ALUMNI AND HIGHER EDUCATION:
A SURVEY OF COLLEGE GRADUATES
Joe L. Spaeth and Andrew M. Greeley

CHANGE IN EDUCATIONAL POLICY:
SELF-STUDIES IN SELECTED COLLEGES AND UNIVERSITIES
Dwight R. Ladd

STATE OFFICIALS AND HIGHER EDUCATION:
A SURVEY OF THE OPINIONS AND EXPECTATIONS OF POLICY MAKERS IN NINE STATES
Heinz Eulau and Harold Quinley

ACADEMIC DEGREE STRUCTURES:
INNOVATIVE APPROACHES
PRINCIPLES OF REFORM IN DEGREE STRUCTURES IN THE UNITED STATES
Stephen H. Spurr

COLLEGES OF THE FORGOTTEN AMERICANS:
A PROFILE OF STATE COLLEGES AND REGIONAL UNIVERSITIES
E. Alden Dunham

FROM BACKWATER TO MAINSTREAM:
A PROFILE OF CATHOLIC HIGHER EDUCATION
Andrew M. Greeley

THE ECONOMICS OF THE MAJOR PRIVATE UNIVERSITIES
William G. Bowen
(Out of print, but available from University Microfilms.)

THE FINANCE OF HIGHER EDUCATION
Howard R. Bowen
(Out of print, but available from University Microfilms.)

ALTERNATIVE METHODS OF FEDERAL FUNDING FOR HIGHER EDUCATION
Ron Wolk

INVENTORY OF CURRENT RESEARCH ON HIGHER EDUCATION 1968
Dale M. Heckman and Warren Bryan Martin

The following technical reports are available from the Carnegie Commission on Higher Education, 1947 Center Street, Berkeley, California 94704.

RESOURCE USE IN HIGHER EDUCATION:
TRENDS IN OUTPUT AND INPUTS, 1930 to 1967
June O'Neill

TRENDS AND PROJECTIONS OF PHYSI-CIANS IN THE UNITED STATES'1967-2002
Mark S. Blumberg

MAY 1970: THE CAMPUS AFTERMATH OF CAMBODIA AND KENT STATE
Richard E. Peterson and John Bilorusky

The following reprints are available from the Carnegie Commission on Higher Education, 1947 Center Street, Berkeley, California 94704. (First copies of reprints are sent free on request. Enclose 20 cents for additional copies to defray costs of postage and handling).

SCIENTIFIC MANPOWER 1970-1985, *by Allan M. Cartter, reprinted from SCIENCE, vol. 172, April 9, 1971.*

A NEW METHOD OF MEASURING STATES' HIGHER EDUCATION BUR-DEN, *by Neil H. Timm, reprinted from* THE JOURNAL OF HIGHER EDUCATION, *vol. xlii, no. 1, January 1, 1971.*

REGENT WATCHING, *by Earl F. Cheit, reprinted from* AGB REPORTS, *vol. 13, no. 6, March 1971.*

THE DIVIDED PROFESSORIATE, *by Seymour M. Lipset and Everett C. Ladd, Jr., reprinted from* CHANGE, *vol. 3, no. 3, May-June 1971.*

THE POLITICS OF AMERICAN POLITICAL SCIENTISTS, *by Everett C. Ladd, Jr., and Seymour M. Lipset, reprinted from* P S, *vol. iv, no. 2, Spring 1971.*

. . . AND WHAT PROFESSORS THINK: ABOUT STUDENT PROTEST AND MAN-NERS, MORALS, POLITICS, AND CHAOS ON THE CAMPUS, *by Seymour Martin Lipset and Everett Carll Ladd, Jr. reprinted from* PSYCHOLOGY TODAY, *November 1970.*

DEMAND AND SUPPLY IN U.S. HIGHER EDUCATION: A PROGRESS REPORT, *by Roy Radner and Leonard S. Miller, reprinted from* AMERICAN ECONOMIC REVIEW, *May 1970.*

THE UNHOLY ALLIANCE AGAINST THE CAMPUS, *by Kenneth Keniston and Michael Lerner, reprinted from* NEW YORK TIMES MAGAZINE, *November 8, 1970, pp. 28-86.*

PRECARIOUS PROFESSORS: NEW PATTERNS OF REPRESENTATION, *by Joseph W. Garbarino, reprinted from* IN-DUSTRIAL RELATIONS, *vol. 10, no. 1, February 1971.*

RESOURCES FOR HIGHER EDUCATION: AN ECONOMIST'S VIEW, *by Theodore W. Schultz, reprinted from* JOURNAL OF POLITICAL ECONOMY, *vol. 76, no. 3, University of Chicago, May/June 1968.* *

INDUSTRIAL RELATIONS AND UNIVER-SITY RELATIONS, *by Clark Kerr, reprinted from* PROCEEDINGS OF THE 21st ANNUAL WINTER MEETING OF THE INDUSTRIAL RELATIONS RESEARCH ASSOCIATION, *pp. 15-25.* *

NEW CHALLENGES TO THE COLLEGE AND UNIVERSITY, *by Clark Kerr, reprinted from Kermit Gordon (ed.),* AGENDA FOR THE NATION, *The Brookings Institution, Washington, D.C., 1968.* *

PRESIDENTIAL DISCONTENT, *by Clark Kerr, reprinted from David C. Nichols* (ed.), PERSPECTIVES ON CAMPUS TENSIONS: PAPERS PREPARED FOR THE SPECIAL COMMITTEE ON CAMPUS TENSIONS, *American Council on Education, Washington, D.C., September 1970.* *

STUDENT PROTEST– AN INSTITUTIONAL AND NATIONAL PROFILE, *by Harold Hodgkinson, reprinted from* THE RECORD, *vol. 71, no. 4, May 1970.* *

WHAT'S BUGGING THE STUDENTS?, *by Kenneth Keniston, reprinted from* EDUCA-TIONAL RECORD, *American Council on Education, Washington, D.C., Spring 1970.* *

THE POLITICS OF ACADEMIA, *by Seymour Martin Lipset, reprinted from David C. Nichols* (ed.), PERSPECTIVES ON CAMPUS TEN-SIONS: PAPERS PRESENTED FOR THE SPE-CIAL COMMITTEE ON CAMPUS TENSIONS, *American Council on Education, Washington, D.C., September 1970.* *

*Out of stock.

May 1970

May 1970:

THE CAMPUS AFTERMATH OF CAMBODIA AND KENT STATE

by *Richard E. Peterson*

Research Psychologist,
Educational Testing Service, Berkeley

and *John A. Bilorusky*

Senior Research Associate,
Institute for Research and Training in Higher Education,
University of Cincinnati

A Technical Report Sponsored by
The Carnegie Commission on Higher Education

The Carnegie Commission on Higher Education,
1947 Center Street, Berkeley, California 94704,
has sponsored preparation of this profile as a
part of a continuing effort to obtain and present
significant information for public discussion.
The views expressed are those of the authors.

MAY 1970

The Campus Aftermath of Cambodia and Kent State

Contents

Foreword

Campus turmoil is almost certainly not solely a thing of the past. But the climax of dissent, disruption, and tragedy in all American history to date occurred in May 1970. That month saw the involvement of students and institutions in protests in greater number than ever before in history. The variety of protest activities—both violent and nonviolent—seemed to exhaust the entire known repertoire of forms of dissent.

In this study, Richard Peterson sent questionnaires to the presidents of 2,551 colleges and universities to determine exactly what happened, and what impacts the events of this critical month are likely to have. He received a remarkable 73 percent response. A generalized summary of his findings are in the table below:

Intensity of the Spring 1970 Upheaval in Various Types of Colleges

	N	Student/ staff strike: one day or longer	Student efforts to communicate with local people about the war	Essentially peaceful demonstrations	Demonstrations damaging persons or property
Type and Level of Institution					
Independent universities	37	41%	89%	89%	16%
Public universities	114	28	71	76	28
Indep. 4-year colleges	198	27	61	62	3
Public 4-year colleges	255	13	45	54	5
Catholic institutions	227	10	37	41	2
Protestant institutions	338	7	35	38	1
Public junior colleges	477	8	27	32	1
Selectivity (4-year institutions only)					
Freshmen mostly from top 10% of H.S. class	135	35	80	79	9

Intensity of the Spring 1970 Upheaval in Various Types of Colleges *continued*

	N	*Student/ staff strike: one day or longer*	*Student efforts to communicate with local people about the war*	*Essentially peaceful demonstrations*	*Demonstrations damaging persons or property*
Selectivity (4-year institutions only) continued					
Mostly from top 40%	598	16	53	58	6
Essentially open admissions	297	9	33	41	5
Enrollment					
More than 12,000	138	29	69	75	30
5,000 to 12,000	231	17	54	67	7
1,000 to 5,000	757	13	42	48	2
Less than 1,000	722	10	29	28	less than 1
Region					
Northeast	468	29	61	62	4
Pacific States	238	19	56	54	5
Midwest	621	12	34	39	4.5
Mountain States	82	7	30	39	4
Southeast	445	7	20	29	2
"Federal Grant Universities"	49	33	84	84	31

Dr: Peterson's presentation and analysis of these and other data provide not only an instructive view of what happened on the nation's campuses in the spring of 1970, but also some useful suggestions about ways in which the tragedies that marked that era can be avoided in the future. The Carnegie Commission on Higher Education agrees with his conclusion that May 1970 might occur again. But our colleges and universities need not muddle through each successive crisis. Our report, *Dissent and Disruption: Proposals for Consideration by the Campus*, is intended to assist policy making in this difficult and sensitive area. While our recommendations in that and other reports are at certain points divergent from Dr. Peterson's own concluding suggestions, his report makes an important contribution to the understanding of the volatile character of the nation's campuses at the present time.

John Bilorusky makes a similar contribution by concentrating on what happened at a single institution—the University of California at Berkeley. His subject is "reconstitution," the term employed, particularly at Berkeley but also nationally, to describe the generally temporary but occasionally permanent alterations of the institutional character and life of colleges and universities in May 1970 and immediately succeeding months. By analyzing the different kinds of reactions of both individuals and campus departments, Bilorusky helps us to understand not just the diversity found on a large campus, but also gives us a new picture of the difficulty with which such a campus can act in true unity.

Mr. Bilorusky was a graduate student at the University of California in May 1970 and was deeply involved in many of the reconstitution activities. Indeed, he considers his report itself, and the work he undertook to complete it, a contribution to the reconstitution effort. The intensity of his commitment will be evident to his readers, and will make his observations and conclusions of special interest.

Clark Kerr

Chairman
Carnegie Commission
on Higher Education

September 1971

Preface

It was the first week of May 1970. American ground forces were moving through the jungles of Cambodia; four students had been shot to death at Kent State University; and the nation's academic community was responding with a mass expression of outrage. In a small way, the two of us, as individuals, were also part of that reaction. We were also social researchers who, along with many others, sought at the time to alter professional activities in the light of personal beliefs about the urgencies of the time.

Peterson's inclination was to try to gain a sense of the broad sweep of the upheaval on the campuses. A surveyor by disposition and aptitude, his way was to skim off a modicum of information about what happened in May from as many colleges as there were presidents willing to fill out his questionnaire.

Bilorusky's style was to probe more deeply, almost as a clinician, in an attempt to examine the educational and social implications of the protest movement on one campus. The "reconstitution" at Berkeley, perhaps not surprisingly, was a kind of microcosm, embracing many of the sentiments and activities found on other campuses during the month.

Peterson wishes to acknowledge helpful advice from ETS colleagues Abraham Carp and Jonathan Warren; from John Bilorusky, Natalie Gumas, and Jerry Gaff of the Center for Research and Development in Higher Education; and from Clark Kerr, Verne Stadtman, Terry Allen, and Margaret Cheney of the Carnegie Commission staff. Data processing and analyses were carried out by Bruce Kramer and Elaine Burnell. Coding the open-ended answers in the survey was the work of Barbara Wagner, assisted by Marcia Nelson. Pamela Roelfs helped on additional statistical analysis. Vesta Cummings and Patti Kramer typed draft manuscripts. Special thanks, finally, are extended to the 1,856 presidents or their proxies who took the time to fill out the survey questionnaire.

Bilorusky wishes to give a special acknowledgement to Anita Medal for assistance in the critical data analysis stage. Her ideas on and critiques of possible interpretations of the rather complicated interview data were invaluable. He wishes also to thank Katy Jako, Paul Heist, and Nancy Kuriloff for assistance in developing the research design; Terry Lunsford and Harold Hodgkinson for helpful advice regarding data analysis; Linda Anthenien, Jim Barker, Linda Stutler Bowen, Connie Brainard, Anita Castellini, Kathryn Condon, Ricki Dienst, Natalie Gumas, Jan Harris, Millie Henry, Katy Jako, Susan Johnson, Debbie Jones, Betty Kaiser, Susan Louie, Sheila Lydon, Anita Medal, Karen Montgomery, Barry Morstain, Gail Rubman, Jack Scott, Nancy Seifert, Gar Smith, Hildie Spritzer, Sophia Tallen, Stella Welty for assistance in conducting interviews and participant-observations; Richard Peterson, Terry Lunsford, Warren Martin, Paul Heist, Emily Reed, Connie Brainard, Millie Henry, and Jeff Koon for commenting on his initial draft; and Dennis Wynn and Verne Stadtman for editorial assistance. Thanks also go to the some 200 students, professors, and staff who were willing to be interviewed concerning their feelings about events on the campus at the time.

Bilorusky is also indebted to the Center for Research and Development in Higher Education for allowing Anita Medal and him to take time away from their normal duties at the center to work on this study of the reconstitution at Berkeley.

We both are indebted to the Carnegie Commission for supporting the studies that led to this report. We hope our work will give readers perspective on what happened in the academic world in reaction to the events of Cambodia and Kent State, as well as insight into the aspirations that many people on the campuses have about life in academe, and in American society.

Richard E. Peterson
John A. Bilorusky

Berkeley, California
September 1971

Part One

The National Campus Reaction to Cambodia and Kent State: Themes and Variations

1. Turmoil in May

You are there. You're part of the largest, most comprehensive and militant act by American students and faculty in the history of the Republic.

Leo Marx, speaking before the Amherst convocation, was right. By all odds, the protest that broke across the campuses early in May of 1970 was the most massive expression ever of American college student discontent.

The events that led to the upheaval are almost too well known to need recapitulation: the President's unexpected announcement on April 30 that American and South Vietnamese ground forces were moving against enemy sanctuaries in Cambodia; the killing of four students and the wounding of nine others by National Guardsmen at Kent State University in Ohio on May 4; the killing of two students and the wounding of 12 by police at Jackson State College in Mississippi on May 14.

For hundreds of thousands, even millions, of students, faculty, and staff at more than half of the nation's colleges, "business-as-usual" became unthinkable. It was a mass uprising, embracing many more "moderate" than "radical" students; in consequence, the protests were overwhelmingly peaceful and legal, though by no means invariably so. The reaction at first was largely political—an expression of opposition to a policy of the national government. With the Kent State shootings, a powerful emotional response added new fuel and great numbers to the growing turmoil. The killings at Jackson then served to broaden the protest beyond its initial focus on the war. Throughout the uprising there was exhilaration from doing something personally significant, taking control of events, achieving solidarity and community. All these beliefs and emotions came together on the campuses to make for a period of unparalleled antagonism to the political-social order and unprecedented renunciation of academic normalcy.

THE SETTING Cambodia, Kent, Jackson, staggering events as they were, are not sufficient to explain the turbulence that followed them. There had to be a
mood, a frame of mind, a readiness. Of course there was such a climate,
the culmination of close to a decade of widening estrangement and
open conflict between youth culture and established authority.

The temper at many colleges and universities in April 1970 was
tense, ugly, expectant. People on the campuses knew they were into the
"riot season." Violence was continuing at Stanford and Santa Barbara
(a student was shot to death in April in the Isla Vista district there).
The pace quickened as April wore on: assaults on ROTC facilities at
Berkeley and Eugene (Oregon), arson at Penn State, Vietnam moratorium mass marches in several cities on April 15—escalating into violence in Cambridge and Washington, D.C., a prolonged confrontation at
Ohio State University, the perilous days at Yale before and during the
May Day demonstrations protesting an impending trial of Black Panthers. People at many colleges and universities were wondering if their
campus would be the next to undergo the ordeals that Columbia, Harvard, Berkeley, and other campuses had undergone in earlier springs.

THE REACTION The response from the colleges to the President's announcement of the
incursion into Cambodia was instantaneous. Princeton, Rutgers, and
Oberlin mounted demonstrations that very night. Within three days,
calls for massive nationwide demonstrations came from Yale May Day
spokesmen, the National Student Association, The Student Mobilization
Committee, and the then recently disbanded Vietnam Moratorium
Committee. A National Student Strike Information Center was set up
at Brandeis University, which by May 5 was reporting that 135 colleges
had closed down.

People on the campuses who opposed the Vietnam War felt that the
President had deceived them, that the hated war, instead of being
wound down, was to be expanded. How, it was asked, could this new
military thrust possibly be consistent with the proclaimed policy of
ending the conflict that over the years had so divided the country and
so drained the nation's human and material resources? And why, given
the tenor of the times, was the invasion announced with no prior warn-
ing and no prior public discussion?

What happened at Kent State will not soon pass from the national
conscience. How else but as tragedy can one describe the spectacle of
American youths dead at the hands of other American youth, albeit
uniformed ones. The news and the photographs stunned the campuses,
infusing the expanding protest with new elements of shock, outrage,
and profound sadness. Many people saw Kent State as symptomatic of
something vaguely but terribly wrong with American life. Some saw it
more narrowly as evidence of an expanding repression in the country.

For many young people, the meaning of Kent State was personal; those slain were students like themselves, and they could just as well have died at Minnesota, or Texas, or just about anywhere.

Kent State aroused huge numbers of normally inactive students and gave the overall upheaval its mass character. Involvement of many moderates, who had little stomach for radical rhetoric and tactics, led to a general de-escalation of tactics during the balance of the month. This moderation was reminiscent of the entirely peaceful October 1969 Vietnam Moratorium Day, which was probably the largest single expression of student opposition to the war prior to the spring of 1970.

The shootings at Jackson State did not trigger any significant unswing in active protest nationally.[1] Overt reactions seemed to be limited to black colleges; Howard University, Lincoln University (Pennsylvania), and Paine College (Augusta, Georgia), for example, suspended normal operations for the rest of the term. There were demonstrations at Morgan State and Bowie State in Maryland. On May 20, a group of 15 black college presidents went to Washington, D.C. together to communicate their concern to the White House. After the Jackson State killings, President James Cheek of Howard University observed that black student resentment was near the "breaking point" (*Chronicle of Higher Education*, May 25, 1970).

On the predominately white campuses, the effect of Jackson State was to move the overwhelmingly white protestors somewhat away from their preoccupation with Indochina and the whites slain at Kent. Under pressure from the small contingents of blacks at these colleges, white students were reminded that racism was a continuing fact in the land, and that young blacks were being killed and wounded by civil authorities in rather greater numbers than whites.[2]

Protest leaders generally stressed that actions were directed at national government rather than at the universities. Yet the campus was the locale of most of the protest, and at hundreds of institutions the outbreak was so massive that college authorities were powerless to take countering action. Typically, it was not a matter of countering force with force; when students and professors decide they no longer want to learn and teach as usual, no number of policemen or National Guardsmen, let alone administrators' exhortations, will make them do so. Strong actions to stem the tide would have been futile at best and, at worst, would have triggered more desperate confrontation. Such was the intensity of the upheaval.

[1] A conclusion from studies by the Urban Research Corporation (1970b) and the American Council on Education (Astin, 1971).

[2] Three black students were killed and 34 wounded by state police in Orangeburg, S.C., on February 8, 1968; six blacks were slain and 20 wounded by police in Augusta, Ga., on May 12, 1970.

Expressions of protest across the country took every conceivable form and were carried out under every conceivable banner, slogan, and cry. There were strikes, boycotts, and shutdowns; there were marches, rallies, and campuswide convocations; there were flag-lowerings, black armbands, memorial services, vigils, and symbolic funerals; there were special seminars, teach-ins, workshops, and research projects. There were students talking to residents in their homes and where they worked, and there were invitations to the public to come to the campus and talk. Untold numbers of letters and telegrams were sent to public officials. Thousands of campus emissaries went to Washington, D.C. Students worked in congressional primaries, planned for summer campaign work, and pressured for a fall campaign recess. Faculties, presidents, and institutions took stands against the war. All manner of departures from regular academic routines were introduced, including cancelled classes, "reconstituted" classes, entirely new classes,[3] different grading systems (for example, credit/no-credit), grades given for work completed to April 30, and no grades. A substantial number of institutions experienced more extreme or desperate actions, such as assaults on ROTC facilities, sacking of administrative offices, trashing of business and government property near the campus, and threats to professors in their classrooms and offices.[4]

CAMPUS AND STATE IN 1970
Cambodia, Kent, and Jackson triggered a period of perhaps unparalleled strife between the academic community and the national government. In a congressional election year in which campus disorder was a major campaign issue, relations between the university and the Republican administration already had been seriously strained by the time of the Cambodia announcement. The ensuing nine months (May 1970 through January 1971) will be recorded as one of the most remarkable intervals in the history of campus-government—especially campus-White House—relations.

Consider the following partial chronology:

April 28:   Vice-President Agnew, in a Florida fund-raising speech, calls for an end to "appeasement" on the campuses; criticizes professors; attacks university presidents Brewster and Fleming.

[3] A "parallel" New University came into being at Northwestern.

[4] Perhaps the most useful campus-by-campus description of protest activities is contained in the Urban Research Corporation (URC) report entitled *On Strike... Shut It Down!*, dated May 1970. In the meantime, a number of often vivid accounts of the unfolding drama at particular colleges have appeared (all dated 1970). Thomas Cottle has written about Northwestern, the University of Chicago, and the Chicago Circle campus of the University of Illinois; Benjamin DeMott about Amherst; Diamond and Nell about The New School; Samuel Krislov about the University of Minnesota; Lawrence Stone about Princeton; Jack Swenson about Cañada. In addition to the special report on Kent State issued by the Scranton Commission, at least two book-length accounts of events on that campus have appeared (Stone, 1970; Michener, 1971).

April 30:   President Nixon announces invasion of Cambodia.

May 1:   President refers to campus activists as "these bums . . .
blowing up the campuses."

May 1-3:   Immediate nationwide protests against the Cambodia
action called for by Yale May Day spokesmen, the National Student
Association, the Student Mobilization Committee, and the then-
defunct Vietnam Moratorium Committee. National Student Strike
Information Center established at Brandeis; reports 135 colleges
closed down by May 5.

May 4:   Kent State shootings; National Guardsmen kill four
students, wound nine.

May 6:   Letter from Interior Secretary Hickel to the President
leaked; criticizes the Vice-President and Administration insensitivity
to student concerns.

May 8:   President meets with eight Association of American
University presidents; gives assurances in TV news conference that
Administration officials would tone down their speeches about the
colleges.

President appoints Vanderbilt Chancellor Alexander Heard as campus advisor—to interpret "the views and sentiments of the campuses
around the country."

May 9:   Mass (75,000) antiwar demonstration in Washington,
D.C.

May 11:   President meets with 46 state governors to discuss the
campus situation; announces need for better communication with
the colleges.

May 14:   Jackson State shootings: police kill two students,
wound twelve.

May 20:   Presidents of 15 predominantly black colleges meet
with the President to express the anger and frustration of blacks.

May 21:   Education Commissioner James Allen, in a meeting
with United states Office of Education employees, speaks of "the
disastrous effect that this (the Cambodia) action has had on education throughout the country."

May 22:   President appoints Howard University President James
Cheek as special advisor on problems at black colleges.

June 3:   Vice-President, at West Point commencement, condemns youthful radicals and "criminal misfits."

June 10:   Commissioner Allen fired by the President.

June 13:   President announces appointment of nine-man President's Commission on Campus Unrest (PCCU), chaired by former
Pennsylvania Governor William Scranton.

June 16:   Vice-President calls for resignation of Joseph Rhodes,
liberal black student member of the PCCU.

July 23:   Advisors Heard and Cheek file their report: indicate gravity of problems at both white and black colleges; stress extent of opposition to the national government on the campuses.

July 30:   President, in a TV news conference, indicates, in reference to the Heard-Cheek memo, placing primary blame for campus unrest on the Government is "short-sighted."

September 1:   McGovern-Hatfield proposal (to cut off funds for Vietnam and set a definite timetable for troop withdrawal), widely supported by students, rejected by the Senate.

September 16: President, in an address at Kansas State University, condemns violence and terror, minimizes government policies as a cause of campus unrest, stresses the need for stronger actions by college administrators.

September 18: Presidential letter sent to 975 college presidents emphasizes that college communities are responsible for "order and discipline" on their campuses.

September 22: President asks Congress to authorize 1,000 FBI agents for investigating campus bombings.

September 23: Vice-President, on the David Frost Show, criticizes college administrators' permissiveness.

September 26: Report of the PCCU transmitted to the White House; calls for an end to violence, renewed understanding, "reconciling moral leadership" from the President; report generally received favorably outside governmental circles; Vice-President critical, calls report "pablum for permissiveness."

October 1:   PCCU issues special report on Jackson State: shootings termed an "unreasonable, unjustifiable overreaction."

October 4:   PCCU issues special report on Kent State: criticizes both students and Guardsmen; recommends against using lethal weapons in controlling riots.

October 14:   New York City Small Claims Court rules New York University must return part of a student's tuition because of classes cancelled in May.

House Internal Security Committee releases list of 65 "radical and/or revolutionary" campus speakers.

October 16:   Special Ohio grand jury indicts 25 at Kent; places major blame on university administrators; exonerates National Guard.

October 29:   Justice Department/FBI report on Kent State released; notes that Guardsmen were not "in a shooting situation."

President, in a speech at San Jose (California) decries violence and speaks of the need for law and order; presidential limousine allegedly stoned.

October 31:   President, in a speech at Phoenix, speaks of "thugs and hoodlums" ... the result of "appeasement," "creeping permissiveness ... in our universities"; speech televised on election eve.

November 3:   The national elections.

November 25:   Secretary Hickel fired.

January 8:   President, in a TV interview with network corre-
spondents, indicates that "the tragedies at Kent . . . Jackson . . . Wis-
consin" constitute the "greatest disappointment" of his first two
years as President.

January 12:   Presidential reply to the report of the PCCU; letter to
Chairman Scranton is thoughtful and generally conciliatory; notes
that the "work of the Commission has expanded our understanding."

January 14:   President, in an address to students at the University of
Nebraska, calls for reconciliation between the generations: "there
has been too much of a tendency of many of my generation to
blame all your generation for the excesses of a violent few." "Our
priorities are really the same." "I pledge to you that as you have
faith in our intentions, we will do our best to keep faith with your
hopes. . ."

January 22:   State of the Union Message: the President, proposing
important substantive and structural changes, calls for "a new American revolution in which power [is] turned back to the people."

Mr. Nixon and his advisors very likely knew that the Cambodia
decision would evoke an outcry from the academic world. What was
not anticipated, and probably could not have been, were the events at
Kent and Jackson and that instead of a predictable reaction from the
radical and activist 5 percent of the academic community, there would
be an outpouring of opposition embracing perhaps half of the total
college population (students, faculty, and staff). By the end of the
second week of May, and after some 500 colleges had shut down temporarily or until the end of the term, the White House realized that it
must, in some degree, improve relations with the campuses. This stance
of solicitude lasted approximately a month—through the appointment
of the Scranton Commission on June 13. The White House then
resumed its critical attitude toward the colleges. During the ensuing five
months, as the November election drew near, the public utterances
from the White House and many Republican (and Democratic) candidates about college students, the "situation on the campuses," and law
and order grew increasingly condemnatory and divisive. In California,
for example, the choice, according to the Senate incumbent, was
between "law and order" and "anarchy."

The major turning point in this brief history came with the
November elections. Law-and-order candidates generally failed to win
election, and it became clear to most observers that the politics of
divisiveness and fear had, for the most part, been counterproductive.
Early in January, the President's thoughtful, appreciative letter of reply

to William Scranton, chairman of the President's Commission on Campus Unrest, was drafted and delivered. Mr. Nixon's January 14 speech at the University of Nebraska was clearly conciliatory. Finally, as this is being written, the President has given this State of the Union Message (described by Columnist James Reston of the *New York Times* as "generous, idealistic and optimistic") with its unmistakable overtures to the nation's dissatisfied youth. The stance in official Washington had shifted from harsh criticism of the universities, to ostensive solicitude, then back to rancor and divisiveness, and finally to appeals for unity and a peaceful "revolution"—all within a most memorable nine-month period.[5]

[5]That the seeming moderation of the White House posture after the election did *not* mean an early scaling down of Indochina military operations is evidenced by the U.S.-supported incursion into Laos, planning for which must have antedated the actual invasion (February 8) by some weeks or months.

2. Survey Method

Information about the national campus reaction to Cambodia/Kent/ Jackson was gathered through a questionnaire sent in July 1970 to all college and university presidents in the country. The questionnaire, which is reproduced in the Appendix, was relatively brief, consisting for the most part of questions answerable with checkmarks only.[1] The presidents were asked whether or not various kinds of activities, such as a letter-writing campaign or a student/faculty strike, occurred in response to the Cambodia announcement or the Kent or Jackson State killings. In addition, nine open-ended questions solicited judgments and interpretations about matters not readily amenable to checkmark or multiple-choice answers. Answers to these questions, which varied to the point of idiosyncrasy, required coding into manageable numbers of general response themes.[2]

The decision to survey presidents and no other campus representatives was prompted chiefly by our desire to carry out the survey while the events of the spring were still fresh in the minds of the people involved—and then to make the resulting information generally available as rapidly as possible.[3] Questionnaires, in short, needed to go out during the summer months and we concluded that presidents (or assistants) generally would be available to complete the form during late July and August, while a designated faculty member or student respondent might not.

It is well known that college policies and operations are often perceived differently by different campus constituent groups (Williamson

[1] Seven of these, the first block of items on the form, solicited institutional characteristics, such as size, regional location, and so forth.

[2] Two coders read every open-ended answer. Disagreements between coders regarding category assignments were resolved by the writer. The number of response categories per question ranged up to 26 (judged necessary to meaningfully code the extreme variety of answers to the last question on the form).

[3] A brief summary of the findings was sent to all the presidents in early October 1970.

& Cowan, 1966; Peterson, Centra, Hartnett, & Linn, 1970). In the Urban Institute study of campus unrest (Buchanan & Brackett, 1970), student government presidents, compared to college presidents and faculty spokesmen, perceived greater student and faculty participation in post-Cambodia demonstrations, and the student respondents also more often believed the post-Cambodia unrest to have been more serious than the unrest prior to the Cambodia invasion. It is important to realize that such differences exist, and to keep in mind that the basic data for this study are college presidents' perceptions of what transpired on their respective campuses during May in reaction to Cambodia/Kent/Jackson.

SAMPLE
September 5, some six weeks after the original mailing, was the date when statistical analyses were begun.[4] By then, 1,856 of the questionnaires had been returned. Using 2,551 (USOE, 1970) as the total number of institutions in the population, the response rate was 73 percent.

An important question in any mail survey, of course, concerns the representativeness of the sample. A partial answer is given in Table 1.

Sample variations from regional populations are generally small. The Pacific and Mountain States, where response rates were relatively high, account for relatively small proportions of the total spectrum. Higher return rates in the West probably reflect the fact that there are higher proportions of public institutions in the Western states.

There was a substantial difference in return rates from public and private sectors, with the result that public institutions are somewhat overrepresented in the sample, and the private institutions, particularly the independent (nonsectarian) ones, are somewhat underrepresented. The proportions of public and private institutions in the country in 1969-70, according to USOE, were 42.3 percent and 57.3 percent respectively; in the survey sample, the proportions are 48.5 percent and 51.2 percent.

Public institutions tend to be larger than the private colleges and more often have year-round operations. Thus their chief executives or proxies are more likely to be on hand during the summer months.

Institutions in the public sector are broken down by degree level for the population and the sample in Table 2. The data are more suggestive than definitive because the classifications of colleges by level used by the USOE and the classifications used in the present survey are not entirely comparable. At the least, it can be said that the public two-year colleges are near to being correctly represented in the sample, and that the public four-year colleges, especially, and the public universities, to a

[4]A single "broadcast" follow-up postcard was sent out during the first week of August.

TABLE 1   Selected population* and sample statistics

	N in population	N in sample	Return rate	Percent in population	Percent in sample
Control or affiliation					
Public	1,079	901	84%	42.3%	48.5%
Private	1,472	951	65	57.7	51.2
Independent	637	371	58	25.0	20.0
Catholic	318	227	71	12.5	12.2
Protestant	486	338	70	19.1	18.2
Other private	31	15	48	1.2	0.8
Question not answered		4			0.2
Regional location†					
Northeast	650	468	72%	25.5%	25.2%
Southeast	638	445	70	25.0	24.0
Midwest	860	621	72	33.8	33.5
Mountain	103	82	80	4.0	4.4
Pacific	282	235	83	11.1	12.7
Outside continental USA	18	3	17	0.7	0.2

*SOURCE: *USOE Higher Education Directory, 1969-1970,* 1970.
† For states comprising each region, see questionnaire item 6 (Appendix).

TABLE 2   Population* and sample statistics for public institutions

	N in population	N in sample	Return rate	Percent in population	Percent in sample
All public institutions	1,079	901	84%	42.3%	48.5%
Ph.D.-granting universities	140	114	81	5.5	6.1
Four-year colleges	289†	255‡	88	11.3	13.7
Two-year colleges	650	477	73	25.5	25.7
Professional and other specialized institutions		55			3.0

*SOURCE: *USOE Higher Education Directory, 1969-1970,* 1970.
† Includes all colleges other than two-year and Ph.D.-granting institutions.
‡ Questionnaire item 1, alternatives 2, 3, and 4.

smaller extent, are overrepresented. One notes in passing that the total number of public universities comprises a relatively small fraction—5.5 percent according to the Office of Education directory—of the total range of institutions.

As indicated in Table 1, it is the independent institutions, rather than the church-related colleges within the private sector, that are underrepresented. A classification of independent colleges and universities by degree level is given in Table 3, and again the population and sample comparisons are less than satisfactory. Nonetheless, it seems (1) that the doctoral level institutions are *not* underrepresented, (2) that the independent two-year colleges *are* underrepresented, but that they constitute a small fraction of the total, and (3) that the independent four-year colleges are underrepresented, and that, because of their large numbers, their underrepresentation constitutes a relatively important source of bias in the sample.

TABLE 3   Population* and sample statistics for independent institutions

	N in population	*N in sample*	*Return rate*	*Approximate percent in population*	*Percent in sample*
All independent institutions					
1969-1970	637*	371	58%	25%	20.0%
1967-1968	576			23	
Ph.D-granting institutions	81†			3	
Ph.D-granting non-specialized universities	44 §	37	84	2	2.0
Four-year colleges	357	198	55	14	10.7
Two-year colleges	123	69	56	5	3.7
Professional and other specialized institutions		67‡			3.6
Other	15			1	

*SOURCE: *USOE Higher Education Directory, 1967-1968,* 1968, which gives the most recent breakdown of independent institutions by level.

†*USOE Directory, 1969-1970,* 1970.

‡Includes theological, technical, and other specialized institutions.

§ Count made by the author from the 1967-1968 *Directory.*

INTERPRETIVE
LIMITATIONS

The reader is cautioned again that the basic data for the study are perceptions of college presidents. A typical faculty man would probably report somewhat greater activity, and student representatives would rather definitely report greater activity. From this standpoint, then, the picture(s) to be drawn from the data in this study may be somewhat conservative.

The two main sources of sampling bias—overrepresentation of public four-year institutions, and underrepresentation of independent (nonsectarian) four-year colleges—may operate in roughly equal and counterbalancing fashion. While both groups of colleges experienced a May reaction of greater intensity than all the colleges in the country taken together, the intensity of the protest, we will see, was somewhat stronger (by most indices) at the independent colleges, which numbered somewhat fewer than the four-year public institutions. All in all, the description of the reaction that follows, based on the total sample surveyed, is judged not to be seriously inaccurate for reasons of sample bias.

3. The National Campus Reaction: An Overview

Across the country, some 57 percent of the nation's colleges, according to their presidents, experienced "significant impact"[1] on campus operations as the result of Cambodia, Kent, and Jackson. This means that close to 1,350 of the nation's colleges and universities were in some way stirred by the events of late April and early May. Some 1,200 colleges, 43 percent of the total, were reportedly *un*touched by these events. Students and faculty on what will henceforth be referred to as the *affected* campuses (57 percent of the sample) expressed their concern and outrage in a great many ways.

ESSENTIALLY
UDENT ACTIONS *Peaceful demonstrations* "Essentially peaceful demonstrations" were reported on 44 percent of the nation's campuses,[2] and on 77 percent of the "affected" campuses.[3] These include all the peaceful and usually legal forms of protest that have become associated with the American college scene in the past decade—sit-ins, parades, picketing, mass meetings, rallies, guerilla theatre productions, vigils, and so forth, as well as memorial services for the dead Kent and Jackson State students. Antiwar speakers from off campus put in appearances during May at one in four (26 percent) colleges in the country (no doubt prompting the House Committee on Internal Security to prepare its "blacklist" of radical speakers).

---

[1] Readers should consult the Appendix, which gives the exact wording of the questions used in the survey, as well as the response data for each question for the total sample of presidents.

[2] The 44 percent figure is close to the estimated 42 percent of institutions reporting "protest incidents" of all kinds resulting from Cambodia, Kent, and Jackson in the ACE survey (Astin, 1971). Both figures are higher than the 30 percent of administrators in the Urban Institute survey who reported nonviolent "incidents of campus unrest" after April 30th.

[3] By increasing a given national sample figure by three-quarters, the corresponding figure for the "affected" subsample, the 57 percent indicating some kind of impact on college operations, can be estimated. Both sets of figures are given for every question in the survey in the Appendix.

Communication with local residents One general thrust of the national reaction was that it was a protest directed *not* at the campuses, but at the national government and the prevailing political order. In keeping with this posture, groups of students (and some faculty) at 40 percent of the nation's colleges moved off the campus to talk with individual citizens in their homes and with workers and professionals at their places of work. Typically, students were seeking to arouse seemingly unconcerned citizens to the wrongness of the American presence in Southeast Asia and to the dangers of the President's Cambodia decision; they were also trying to explain to generally bewildered and often hostile citizens what was happening on the campuses, and why. Groups from some colleges journeyed up to 200 miles to talk with people in relatively isolated areas. The students involved in this activity were overwhelmingly moderate and straight, rather than radical or freaky; they were youths with a large measure of respect for the common citizenry. As a form of student activism, such off-campus efforts (unrelated to a specific political campaign) probably represent something quite new. The impact on the minds of the people contacted is unknown; that these profoundly decent and well-meaning activities were a significant dimension of the May reaction, however, cannot be denied.

Special meetings, seminars, projects Thirty-seven percent of the presidents reported that "special seminars, workshops, or research projects were initiated" on their campuses. At many colleges these activities took the place of all or part of the regular academic program; elsewhere they were supplemental. From various accounts, one gains the impression of frenzied activity. Individual courses were "reconstituted" to consider the war, national priorities, and the appropriate university response. At some institutions, departments and other academic subdivisions became the focus for antiwar work. At small colleges, there were often continuing convocations, "dialogues," and the like involving all or almost all the student body. Some classes were cancelled at one in four (25 percent) colleges. Research-minded students and faculty in some departments and centers applied their skills to opinion polling and related kinds of projects on campus, in the local community, and in nearby corporations. One-third (34 percent) of the presidents indicated that physical facilities on their campuses were made available for antiwar work or other political activity.

Letter writing Students and staff on many campuses chose to express themselves by writing personal letters to the White House, anti-Vietnam war senators and congressmen, and other public officials. A number of college presidents wired the White House in behalf of the total college community. Some campuses forwarded letters or petitions signed by hundreds or even thousands of people. "Letter-writing campaigns," however defined, were reported at 29 percent of the colleges.

Political party campaign work Much has been said in the meantime about student intentions (in May) to become involved in campaigns of congressional and other candidates running on end-the-war platforms. The Princeton-based Movement for a New Congress (MNC) was formed in early May, and a computerized network was extended to some 300 colleges. On many of these campuses, students began in May to get organized to work in their home (or other) districts during the summer—especially in districts where MNC analysts had determined there were peace candidates who had a chance. In several Eastern states, students became involved in the spring in a number of primary campaigns (with mixed results). All in all, almost one in four presidents (23 percent) reported some sort of student/staff planning for campaign activities in support of congressional or local peace candidates. The promise for this within-the-system political involvement, as we will see, largely failed to materialize.

Actions at Washington, D.C., and state capitals Another form of expression consisted of carrying the message from the campus directly and personally to federal and state political figures. Groups from one in five (20 percent) colleges in the country travelled to Washington, D.C. to meet with congressmen and otherwise lobby for Indochina de-escalation and other antiwar measures. Perhaps best known was the close to 700-man/woman delegation from Haverford, comprising almost the total college community, led by its president, John Coleman.

Judging from newspaper and other accounts (notably the Urban Research Corporation report), activities in state capitals, in contrast to the personal talking in Washington offices, more often took the form of parades, sit-ins, and other forms of mass demonstration. At any rate, 14 percent of the presidents said that groups from their campuses carried their protest to the state capital.

Shutdowns and strikes Normal instructional activities shut down for a day or longer during May on one-fifth (21 percent, some 536[4]) of the nation's campuses. General student/staff *strikes* reportedly took place at 14 percent of the campuses—in absolute numbers, at roughly 350 colleges and universities.

We interpret a "strike" to mean unilateral student, or student and faculty, action, without administrator or trustee concurrence, to boy-

---

[4]Population estimate.

cott classes and, depending on the type of institution, to impede other institutional functions (such as research activities).

The 21 percent shutdown figure, on the other hand, refers to cessation of the regular instructional program for any and all reasons. Student strikes were undoubtedly either the direct or the indirect cause for many, perhaps half, of the reported shutdowns. Shutdowns reportedly lasted for one day only at 8 percent (205[5]) of the campuses; two-day shutdowns occurred at 7 percent (178) of the colleges; three- to six-day shutdowns, at 3 percent (76); one- to two-week shutdowns, at 1 percent (26); and for the duration of the term,[6] at 2 percent (51) of the campuses. At 17 percent of the colleges, some number of students returned home before the end of the term, with more than 10 percent of the student body leaving at 6 percent of the colleges.

What was involved in the "decision" to shut down? When asked by whose decision or order the shutdown occurred, almost one-third (31 percent) of the presidents said it was by their own order; 14 percent indicated it was by the president with concurrence of the other campus constituent groups; 12 percent said it was a faculty decision; 11 percent said it was by the state governor's order; 26 percent reported various other patterns; and 6 percent gave no answer. Percentage responses to the question, "what were the sources of pressure to close?", were categorized as follows for institutions shut down.[7]

1 Students, 66 percent

2 Faculty, 38 percent

3 Fear of violence or disruptive confrontations, 9 percent

4 Other nearby colleges closing, 7 percent

5 State governor, 7 percent

6 Emotions on campus running high, need for a cooling off, etc., 5 percent

7 Other answers, 4 percent

Violence Demonstrations causing damage to persons or property took place during May on 4 percent (3.9 percent) of the campuses—73 institutions in the sample or about 100 campuses in the country.[8] Four

[5]Population estimate.

[6]May have been less than two weeks.

[7]Multiple answers were sometimes given; percents sum to more than 100.

[8]A slightly lower figure, 2.3 percent, was obtained in the Urban Institute survey; 36 of 1,586 administrators indicated that "incidents of violence occurred, involving serious damage to or destruction of property, personal injury or death" (after May 1, 1970).

percent of the presidents reported that outside law enforcement forces—city or state police, National Guard—were on the campus at some time during the month. Radical, as opposed to "moderate," student/faculty leaders were said to be in command of events on 3 percent of the campuses.

A number of observers, particularly people based on or near campuses that had undergone continued unrest prior to May, noted that the level of violence or law breaking declined noticeably after the Kent State killings—for the reason that large numbers of moderate students who were shunning extreme tactics had become involved. However, on a question in the survey that asked whether "protest on your campus" was "more violent/disruptive/destructive after Cambodia . . . ," 18 percent answered affirmatively, as compared to only 2 percent who responded that protest was "less violent after Cambodia . . ." (19 percent said "no difference"; the rest said "no real protest" either before or after April 30).[9] At places like Berkeley and Stanford, where there had been repeated trashing and student-police confrontations prior to May, post-Cambodia actions seemed relatively temperate, despite the huge amount of activity. Across the country, there was simply an upsurge of campus activism of all kinds—peaceful *and* destructive. While the absolute number of violent acts undoubtedly escalated somewhat after April 30, the ratio of violent to nonviolent behavior probably was not much different before and after. Everything escalated.[10] There was also an increase in protest actions, including destructive ones, *off campus*, which is an aspect of the overall reaction that has not been adequately covered in the other surveys.

Commencement exercises The national news media gave particular attention to what seemed to be widespread breaking with tradition in the conduct of graduation exercises for the class of 1970. In fact, only 7 percent of the presidents indicated that the events of the spring had led to recasting commencement proceedings, usually to do without some of the familiar rituals of order, oratory, and dress. A handful of colleges cancelled graduation exercises entirely. Students engaged in symbolic (nondisruptive) expression of antiwar sentiment (peace symbols on mortar boards) or mourning for the Kent and Jackson State dead (black armbands) during commencement ceremonies at 17 percent

[9] A major conclusion from the Urban Institute survey was that "incidents that occurred . . . after April 30, 1970, were more serious than previous incidents."

[10] In the Urban Institute study, administrators (a 56 percent sample) reported a total of 388 "incidents" of campus unrest throughout the seven or eight months of the 1969-70 academic year up to April 30; during the one or two months left in the year, a total of 508 such "incidents" was reported.

of the colleges. Exercises were actually disrupted in any significant way on fewer than 1 percent of the campuses.

FACULTY AND DEPARTMENTAL ACTIONS

Another major theme of the May uprising was the widespread abnegation of normal academic routines. There had to be, of course, some measure of support for such action from the faculty, who on most campuses exercise effective, if not always formal, authority over academic affairs. Some dimensions of the reponse of faculties nationally, as well as certain implications of this response in the eyes of the presidents, are set forth below.

Across the country, more than one in four presidents (28 percent) indicated that some undergraduate courses were "modified to reflect antiwar interests." At most of these institutions, 18 percent nationally, a rather small number of courses (and professors)—less than 10 percent—were thus "reconstituted." At 6 percent of the colleges, 10 percent to 25 percent of the courses were so modified, and at 4 percent (78 colleges in the sample, roughly 107 in the population), more than one-fourth of undergraduate courses were reconstituted.

Roughly the same picture emerged with regard to faculty modification of final examination and grading procedures. One in four colleges (25 percent) reported deviations from usual procedures, with fairly extensive modification (involving more than 25 percent of the faculty) occurring on 8 to 10 percent of the campuses. Many different systems seemed to have been used, with the scheme of forgoing further exams and allowing students to take grades based on work completed prior to April 30 probably being the most common.

On some campuses, observers were struck by the universality of the campus reaction, by the fact that it involved people from parts of the institution that had theretofore never been known for any kind of political activism. What this usually meant was that students and faculty from certain professional fields—especially engineering and business—had "finally" or "for the first time" become politically engaged. This was indeed the case on the Berkeley campus, as Bilorusky points out. What patterns of "reconstitution activities" by academic field were reported at other colleges and universities across the country?

A general and again partial answer is provided in Table 4, which is based on the presidents' answers to a block of questions about "departures from normal examination and grading procedures" in eight academic and professional fields. The left-hand "N" column gives the number of presidents who gave an answer—either "substantial." "some," or "little or no"—for each academic field. The difference between a given N, e.g., the 736 for Business, and 1,064, the number indicating "impact" in question 8, is the number who gave no answer, meaning either that there was no school of business at the respondent's college, or that for whatever reason the president chose not to answer that particular item. Thus the percentages are based on the numbers responding; percentages total horizontally to 100 (within rounding errors).

TABLE 4 Modification of academic routines in May, by academic field

Question:		"In which academic divisions were there departures from normal examination and grading procedures during May or June?"					
		"Substantial"		"Some"		"Little or no"	
	N	*N*	*Percent*	*N*	*Percent*	*N*	*Percent*
Business	736	51	6.9	62	8.2	623	84.6
Education	761	63	8.2	101	13.3	597	78.4
Engineering	615	36	5.9	38	6.2	541	88.0
Fine arts	822	90	10.9	179	21.8	553	67.3
Humanities	896	125	14.0	249	27.8	522	58.3
Life sciences	826	72	8.7	125	15.1	629	76.2
Physical sciences	853	73	8.6	124	14.5	656	77.0
Social sciences	887	130	14.7	264	29.8	493	55.6

The essential message in Table 4 is perhaps most readily told by the figures in the extreme right-hand column. The higher the percentage, the less often (proportionately) were there deviations from standard examination and grading systems. A rank ordering of academic fields from the most often "reconstituted" (in some degree) to the most often holding the line was: social sciences, humanities, fine arts, life sciences, physical sciences, education, business, engineering.

In general, departmental differences in participation in the May reaction were quite substantial. At some colleges—about 100 or 4 percent of the total—the response was essentially institutionwide. More typically, however, "no business-as-usual" prevailed in the social sciences, humanities, and arts, while business and engineering, insofar as the scheduled instructional program was concerned, carried on pretty much as usual; physical sciences, life sciences, and education—perceived by the presidents to have reacted in roughly similar fashion—occupied the middle ground on the continuum.

That people in various academic disciplines differ in political and social ideology is fairly widely recognized. Probably the best available evidence comes from the 1969 Carnegie Commission-sponsored survey of 60,000 faculty. In an analysis of these data by Lipset and Ladd, the rank ordering of fields of study by proportion of respondents identifying themselves as "left" or "liberal" is exactly the same as the ordering given above. On questions of general support for student activism and opposition to the Vietnam war, the only difference in the rank order was that education stood above the life and physical sciences (Lipset and Ladd, 1970). Another factor is the relative size of or gross number of faculty in the various academic disciplines. Humanities (English, foreign languages, philosophy) is the largest, followed by social sciences and education (roughly tied), physical sciences (including mathematics and statistics), fine arts and life sciences (roughly tied), engineering, and business (Rogers, 1967). The larger the absolute size of the academic division on campus, one may argue, the greater the likelihood there is that the division will have a critical mass of relatively radical and relatively young professors.[11]

Lipset and Ladd were especially impressed by the differences in attitudes by age: "In each discipline, as age increases, support for student activism decreases. It is almost too neat." In the present survey, of the presidents of the 1,064 "affected" colleges, 13 percent indicated that junior (non-tenured) faculty were "much more supportive" of Cambodia reaction activities than senior faculty, 39 percent felt that junior faculty were "somewhat more supportive," while less than 1 percent considered *senior* faculty to have been more supportive (the remainder said there was no difference, or gave no answer).

These differences in faculty values by subject field and age make clear that faculties on most campuses are by no means of one mind. How, one wonders, did the tumult of May affect general faculty unity? From a perspective of two to three months, about half (49 percent) of the presidents of the 1,064 "affected" colleges believed that the May upheaval had had "no significant impact" on the morale and cohesiveness of (the) faculty." Of those presidents who believed that the unity of their faculties *had* been affected, half, again, said the "net impact" had been "greater division and polarization," with the other half (25 percent of the "affected" colleges) believing that the upshot had been "greater unity."

INCIDENTAL ISSUES In the wake of Cambodia/Kent/Jackson, students and staff at many colleges became actively concerned about a variety of issues and problems not directly related to the war in Indochina or the shootings on the two campuses.

Such incidental issues that related to college operations were coded into the six categories listed below. The N is the number of presidents mentioning the issue; the percent is the percentage of the total sample

[11]Many liberal arts colleges, of course, would not have business or engineering departments.

of 1,856 mentioning it: For example, Cambodia/Kent/Jackson sparked critical interest in matters of campus governance on about 9 percent of the nation's campuses.

N	Percent	
163	8.8	Governance and decision making
126	6.7	Curriculum and teaching
46	2.5	Relation of university and society
40	2.2	ROTC*
33	1.8	Appropriate methods of protest and expression of dissent in the university
20	1.1	Parietal rules

Issues bearing on broad social conditions and political affairs that were raised in reaction to Cambodia/Kent/Jackson included the following:

N	Percent	
89	4.8	Racism, racial discrimination†
82	4.4	General issues of war and peace
59	3.2	Environmental pollution, ecology, etc.
52	2.8	Student participation in national political life; 18-year-old vote, campaign work, etc.
46	2.5	Particular aspects of American foreign policy
45	2.4	National priorities in general, poverty in particular
37	2.0	General questions of dissent and repression in American society
24	1.3	The draft
23	1.2	Integrity of governmental institutions, corruption in officials, etc.

PRESIDENTIAL AND INSTITUTIONAL STANDS

Almost one in five (18 percent) of the presidents (or chief campus administrator by some other title) took a public stand, *as an individual*, against the Vietnam war or the Cambodia decision. Five percent of the presidents publicly took a stand of (personal) *neutrality*. And 14 of the 1,856 presidents (less than 1 percent of the sample) took a stand in support of the war or the Cambodia incursion.

*ROTC units existed at 502 institutions in the fall of 1970, with enrollment compulsory at 48 (as against 112 in the fall of 1968) (*New York Times*, December 23, 1970).

†Sixteen percent of the presidents at the "affected" colleges reported some measure of resentment on the part of black students on their campuses about the great outpouring of concern about the war and the killing of *white* students (at Kent State).

More far-reaching in its implications is the act of a college or university, as an institution, taking a position on one side or another on a political issue. Four percent of the colleges and universities in the country, according to their chief executives, took stands—as institutions—in opposition to the Indochina war and the Cambodian incursion. Another 4 percent adopted positions, *qua* institutions, of *neutrality* in regard to the Cambodian action. One president, our computer output told us, said that his college took a stand *in support* of the Cambodia invasion. What it means for a college to take an institutional stand is by no means clear, and the meaning would certainly not be uniform for all of the colleges that took a particular stand. Roughly half the presidents at institutions reportedly taking stands against the Cambodian action said the stand was the result of a faculty vote; in the other half, the decision was reached in some other way, such as through a campuswide referendum.

REACTIONS OF OFF-CAMPUS CONSTITUENCIES

Table 5 gives a general picture of how the presidents perceived the reactions of various constituent groups off campus to the activities on their respective campuses in May. Since destructive actions took place at 7 percent of the "affected" colleges, a critical reaction from at least that percentage of each constituent group (nationally) is probably to be expected.

TABLE 5   Reactions of off-campus constituencies (1,064 "affected" colleges)

Question: "What has been the reaction of particular constituent groups to the various activities of May and June on your campus?"

	"Mainly critical"		"Mainly favorable"		"No discernible reaction"		No response	
	N	Percent	N	Percent	N	Percent	N	Percent
Trustees	184	17.3	483	45.4	318	29.9	79	7.4
Alumni	214	20.1	305	28.7	453	42.6	92	8.6
Parents	180	16.9	323	30.4	475	44.6	86	8.1
Local citizens	321	30.2	297	27.9	367	34.5	79	7.4
State legislators	291	20.6	154	14.5	568	53.4	123	11.6
Local press	139	13.1	402	37.8	427	40.1	96	9.0

One sees, first, that of the six groups considered, local area residents (the "town" of the "town-gown" distinction) were most widely regarded as "mainly critical" of happenings on the campus in May, followed in order by state legislators and alumni (roughly tied), trustees and parents (roughly tied), with the local press least often perceived as having been critical. Because of differences in "no discernable reaction" for the groups, the rank-ordering according to "favorable" reaction is not exactly the reverse of the "critical" ordering. Trustees and the local press were most often regarded as supportive, and state legislators, by a wide margin, least often supportive. It should be noted that state legislators ordinarily are not a relevant constituent group for private institutions, which would be the main reason for the high "no discernable reaction" and no response rates on that item.[12]

IMPLICATIONS:
IN THE
SHORT RUN

Perspectives on academic work A good many people in higher education speak these days of the deterioration of *academic standards*—in the face of student demands for "experiential" and "sensate" learning experiences, for "relevance" to personal lives and contemporary political and social currents, and so forth. "Academic standards," as a concept, is semantically difficult. Let us say that people who use the term usually have reference to mastery of a body of knowledge (as embodied, for example, in a course or group of courses). To the extent, then, that some level of mastery of the predetermined intellectual content of an instructional program is not rigorously pursued by faculty and students, "academic standards" could be said to have declined or "academic integrity" to have been compromised.

Academic standards, thus defined, would seem to have been massively assaulted in May (courses modified at more than one-fourth of the nation's colleges, for example). And, indeed, 18 percent of the presidents (32 percent of the "affected" colleges) said that the impact of Cambodia/Kent/Jackson on academic standards at their campuses had been "detrimental." As will be shown, the judgment of "detrimental" comes heavily, as expected, from presidents of institutions where the reaction was most intense. These institutions also tend to be the places where the general level of academic work is high. Asked about the (continuing) impact of Cambodia on academic standards during the 1970-71 year, the number of presidents fearing it to be "detrimental" dropped by one-half to 9 percent of the total sample (15 percent of the "affected" colleges). Nine percent of 2,551 is 230 colleges, a not insignificant number (even though other people on these campuses may not share the same concern about "standards" as the president).

On the other hand, 4 to 5 percent of the presidents said that the spring upheaval had a "positive" impact on academic standards. What, one wonders, does this response mean?[13] More significantly (and

[12]On this point, a whole different story comes from presidents of public institutions (Table 7).

[13]It might mean that a backlash had set in, that after a brief period of "hysteria," standards would be maintained even more strenuously. Or it may mean that rigid adherence to outmoded ("irrelevant"?) standards of achievement was beginning to break down.

perhaps more readily understood), a substantial number of presidents, one-fourth of those at "affected" colleges, indicated that the spring events had a "positive or beneficial impact on the instructional program on campus." Asked to elaborate in what ways, the answers of these 253 presidents were coded as follows:

1 Increased student/staff concern about curricular reform (28 percent of those who answered).

2 Increased student/faculty/administration cooperation, communication, and understanding of each other's views and problems (24 percent of those who answered).

3 Increased student awareness of and concern about national and international problems (22 percent of those who answered).

4 Increased student concern about broad educational issues (e.g., the nature and role of the university) (21 percent of those who answered).

At the most, these perceptions signify that the May crisis led to a new spirit of community and new impetus for constructive change at better than 1 in 10 colleges in the country. At the least, these data tell us that there are still college presidents possessed of progressivism, optimism, and hope.

Finally, 104 presidents in the sample (the actual number in the country would have been close to 144) said that they anticipated either "some" or "considerable" difficulty in getting the regular academic program going in the fall. To our knowledge, none of the colleges expecting difficulty failed to open on schedule, but this profound uneasiness on the part of a significant number of presidents during the summer is surely symptomatic of the contemporary troubles at many American colleges and universities.

Students and partisan politics Still another important theme of the upheaval was the surge of student interest in helping to elect peace candidates to Congress and other public offices. Planning for such work was reportedly underway at 1 in 4 colleges in May. Indeed, for the liberal press, the prospect of mass student within-the-system political involvement was probably the most important meaning of the May unrest on the campuses. So what happened? Whatever it was, it began early. By midsummer, when our questionnaires were filled out, only 12 percent of the presidents could report that 5 percent or more of their student bodies were currently working for candidates, and less than 1 percent (a total of eight presidents in the sample!) believed that more than 25 percent of their respective student bodies were so involved.

The spring of 1970 saw the invention at Princeton of the "campaign recess." It was a totally new structural form for the campus—an arrangement that would enable, even encourage, large-scale student participation in the established political system. The basic idea was to schedule a one- or two-week break prior to the November elections; under the "Princeton plan" there would be a calendar change so that the lost academic time would be made up through shorter vacations. Born in crisis, the recess idea was first widely hailed, and then—in the wake of Internal Revenue Service and ACE warnings about loss of tax-exempt status—hotly debated.[14] In the middle of the summer, 3 percent of the college presidents reported that there would in fact be campaign recesses at their institutions, with almost three-quarters of these (42 out of 58) indicating that the "Princeton plan" was their model. In addition, 10 percent (190) of the presidents in the sample said a campaign break *was possible,* that the decision had yet to be reached. Extrapolating to the population, some 80 colleges and universities in the country had decided to take campaign recesses, while another 260 were considering the possibility.

A later October survey conducted by the American Council on Education found that only 21 institutions had "scheduled periods when no classes will be held," with breaks (time to be made up later) already underway at nine of the institutions. Additionally, some 300 colleges "are providing no examinations . . . no assignments . . . relaxed attendance policies" (ACE, 1970b).

In sum, as many pre- and post-election newspaper accounts concluded, with the exception of a few scattered campaigns, student involvement in the fall 1970 elections was nowhere near commensurate with the May outpouring of partisan political fervor. In Fred Hechinger's words, "the steam is gone . . ." (*New York Times*, October 25, 1970).

---

[14] Arguments in opposition usually stressed that a campaign recess would be inconsistent with the university's fundamental (educational) mission; that since students would almost always be supporting liberal, radical, antiwar candidates, institutional neutrality would be compromised; and that students would be given a special privilege that other classes of citizens would not enjoy.

4. Scope of the Reaction in Diverse Types of Institutions

In contrast to those in many other countries, American colleges and universities, despite fairly recent pressures to the contrary, are in general highly diverse in their structures, functions, and goals. Indeed, this diversity may be the genius of the sytem.

Some facts[1] In the fall of 1969, close to 8 million students were attending upwards of 2,600 colleges and universities. Forty-two percent of these are public tax-supported institutions; given their typically large size and liberal admissions policies, the public institutions enroll almost three-quarters (73 percent) of the national student population. Some 750 public two-year colleges (fall 1969) with essentially open admissions enroll almost one-quarter of the student population. In the private sector, 486 Protestant-affiliated colleges and 318 Catholic institutions each enroll about 7 percent of all students, with 637 independent colleges and universities accounting for the remaining 15 percent.

Enrollments range from over 30,000 students on one campus, as at several Midwestern state universities, to less than 500 at scores of other schools. There are also huge differences in financial resources, preparation of faculty, academic aptitude of students, and other indices of institutional quality. Roughly one-third of all the colleges are not accredited by a regional accrediting organization. The various kinds of institutions have very different kinds of purposes and programs. Particularly important for the present discussion, colleges across the land also vary enormously in terms of the beliefs, personal values, styles, and commitments of their students, and faculty; life at Berkeley or Harvard is rather different from that at St. John's, Mercer County Community College, or even Penn State.

It is not surprising, therefore, that active student (and faculty) protest in the 1960s has not occurred evenly throughout the spectrum of

---

[1] From U.S.O.E., *Education Directory, Higher Education, 1969-70*; also, as yet unpublished U.S.O.E. opening fall enrollment data for 1969.

American colleges and universities. From its beginning (in the fall of 1964, in Berkeley, let us say), radical student activism has tended to be concentrated in certain types of institutions (Peterson, 1966), and the same pattern, as evidenced by several national surveys, has persisted in the years since—up to and including the spring of 1970. The general explanatory principles are, first, that different kinds of colleges tend to attract, recruit, and enroll different kinds of students, i.e., students with different values and commitments, and, second, that large institutions tend to enroll substantial numbers of *all* kinds of students.[2] The significance of the latter is that at the large university there are likely to be "critical masses" of students interested in engaging in almost any kind of enterprise imaginable—from serious academic work, to trashing ROTC, to liberating jocks.

AT INSTITUTIONS OF VARYING LEVEL AND CONTROL

The typology of institutions employed here was devised to be parsimonious yet cognizant of the important segments of the total spectrum of institutions, comprehensive in covering the total spectrum, and enlightening in terms of the subject and data at hand. Four forms of control—public, independent (of any church), Protestant, and Roman Catholic—and three degree levels—Ph.D., A.B., and A.A., yield 12 categories that would encompass perhaps more than 95 percent of the institutions in the total system. The seven types, as set forth in Tables 6 and 7, embrace 89 percent of the present sample (and presumably of the population of institutions as well).[3] Institutions were classified into the seven categories on the basis of answers to the first two questions in the survey (Table 6).

Table 7 details the scope of the May upheaval at the seven types of institutions on the basis of 18 questions selected from the survey that were selected as descriptive of the main dimensions of the upheaval and its aftermath. The information in the top section of the table serves to describe the institutional types in terms of variables known from previous research to be related to campus political activism; this information will aid in interpreting the substantive data in the table. Next is the general question about whether Cambodia/Kent/Jackson "had . . . significant impact on operations" on the respondent's campus. It was the

[2] Despite seemingly wide adherence to certain youth-as-a-class styles and norms, such as long hair, work clothes, use of marijuana, and so forth, as well as an increasingly aggressive youth-class consciousness, there are still important differences among youth and students in terms of interests, values, and aspirations. One typology of college students (Clark & Trow, 1966) consists of four "subcultures—the collegiate, vocational, academic, and nonconformist." Another (Peterson, 1968b) involves eight types: professionalists, vocationalists, collegiates, ritualists, academics, intellectuals, left-activists, and hippies.

[3] One group of institutions not included in the typology are the 120 independent two-year colleges, where, according to some evidence, student political activism is infrequent (Gaddy, 1970), or nonexistent (Bayer & Astin, 1969).

TABLE 6   Classification of institutions into seven control/level types

	Public university N=114	Public 4-year college N=255	Public 2-year college N=477	Indep. university N=37	Indep. 4-year college N=198	Prot. institution N=338	Catholic institution N=227
Type, level*							
Ph.D-granting university	100.0%			100.0%		2.1%	6.2%
Comprehensive college I: wide range of programs		33.3%			12.1%	5.0	5.7
Comprehensive college II: fewer programs		53.3			17.2	9.8	17.2
4-year liberal arts		13.3			70.7	53.6	51.5
Professional, other specialized school						13.3	5.7
2-year college			100.0			16.0	13.2
Control, affiliation*							
Public	100.0	100.0	100.0				
Independent				100.0	100.0		
Catholic							100.0
Protestant						100.0	

*See Appendix for the exact wording of the questions.

basis for dividing institutions according to whether or not they were "affected" by the events of the spring. In the third section are data on seven kinds of mainly student-initiated actions. Subsequent blocks of data pertain to faculty course-modification actions, presidential and institutional stands, reactions of off-campus constituencies, impact on academic standards, and student political campaign work.

With the exceptions noted at the bottom of the table, all the figures are percentages of the total number of colleges in each category (not the number "affected"); for example, the 76.3 percent for peaceful demonstrations at public universities means that 76 percent of the 114 public university presidents in the sample reported such actions on their campuses. Data for the total sample of 1,856 institutions are given in the left-hand column for purposes of ready comparison.

In general, the reaction was more widespread and intense in independent (nonsectarian) colleges and universities than in public institutions, with the Protestant and Catholic colleges experiencing a much weaker reaction than the nonsectarian colleges. With regard to degree level, the upheaval was strongest in the universities and weakest in the two-year colleges. Thus 97 percent of the nation's independent and 91 percent of the public universities experienced "significant impact on campus operations" from Cambodia/Kent/Jackson. Seventy-seven percent of the independent and 66 percent of the public four-year colleges were likewise "affected." The figures are 55 percent for the Catholic and 52 percent for the Protestant institutions, and 44 percent for the public two-year colleges.

TABLE 7   Cambodia/Kent reaction profiles for seven types of colleges and universities based on institutional control and degree level

	Total sample (N=1,856)	Public university (N=114)	Public 4-year college (N=255)
Institutional factors			
Regional location			
Pacific states	12.8%	10.5%	9.4%
Mountain states	4.4	11.4	5.5
Northeast	25.2	10.5	23.1
Southeast	24.0	27.2	31.0
Midwest	33.5	40.4	30.6
Enrollment			
Less than 1,000	38.9	0.9	5.1
1,000 - 5,000	40.8	4.4	54.9
5,000 - 12,000	12.5	29.0	31.8
More than 12,000	7.4	65.8	7.1
Selectivity			
Top 10% of high school class	8.5	11.4	2.8
Top 40%	39.6	53.5	53.5
Open admissions	50.2	34.2	43.1
Perceived impact			
"Significant impact" on campus operations (i.e., percent "affected")	57.3 (N=1,064)	91.2 (N=104)	65.9 (N=168)

This same pattern tended to hold for the various specific kinds of student actions. Except in the use of violence, students in the independent universities, by substantial margins, were the most widely engaged. Violence occurred at more than one in four (28 percent) of the *public* universities, at 16 percent of the independent universities, and only rarely elsewhere. Strikes reportedly occurred at four in ten (41 percent) of the independent universities, at more than one in four of the public universities (28 percent) and independent colleges (27 percent), and at 13 percent or fewer of the other types of institutions. The public four-year colleges consistently were in an intermediate rank among

Public 2-year college (N=477)	*Indep. uni- versity (N=37)*	*Indep. 4-year college (N=198)*	*Prot. insti- tution (N=338)*	*Catholic insti- tution (N=227)*
23.5%	13.5%	9.6%	10.1%	7.1%
6.5	0.0	3.5	2.1	1.8
15.9	62.2	43.9	9.8	35.7
20.6	10.8	15.7	35.5	15.0
33.5	13.5	26.8	42.6	40.5
28.7	0.0	41.9	63.6	61.7
51.4	29.7	53.0	34.3	31.3
13.8	40.5	4.6	1.8	4.9
5.5	29.7	0.0	0.3	1.8
0.0	54.1	28.3	7.1	6.2
4.8	46.0	50.5	53.6	63.0
95.0	0.0	20.2	37.6	28.6
43.6 (N=208)	97.3 (N=36)	77.3 (N=153)	52.4 (N=177)	55.1 (N=125)

TABLE 7 *continued*

	Total sample (N=1,856)	*Public university (N=114)*	*Public 4-year college (N=255)*
Student initiated actions			
Peaceful demonstrations	44.4	76.3	53.7
Communication with local area residents	40.3	71.1	45.5
Special seminars, workshops, projects, etc.	37.2	67.5	38.0
Planning for electioneering	23.1	50.0	24.7
Shutdown, one day or longer (all reasons)	20.2	34.2	23.5
General student/staff strike, one day or longer	13.6	28.1	12.6
Destructive demonstrations	3.9	28.1	4.7
Modification of instruction			
Some courses modified to reflect antiwar interests	27.9	53.5	32.6
Some faculty modified grading procedures	23.8	55.3	27.8
"Substantial" or "some" departure from normal exam/grading procedures, by academic field:			
Business	6.1	19.5	5.5
Education	8.9	31.0	12.6
Engineering	4.5	11.5	3.1
Fine arts	14.5	38.1	18.8
Humanities	20.2	46.9	22.0
Life sciences	10.6	26.6	12.2
Physical sciences	10.5	25.7	12.2
Social sciences	21.3	48.7	23.1
Anti-Cambodia incursion positions taken			
By the president, as an individual	17.5	28.1	17.3
Institutional stand against the Cambodia invasion	3.9	0.9	6.1

Public 2-year college (N=477)	Indep. uni-versity (N=37)	Indep. 4-year college (N=198)	Prot. insti-tution (N=338)	Catholic insti-tution (N=227)
32.5	89.2	61.6	38.5	41.4
26.6	89.2	61.1	35.2	37.4
25.8	81.1	60.1	31.1	33.0
12.4	62.2	40.4	19.5	19.8
16.8	54.1	30.3	11.2	15.4
7.8	40.5	26.8	7.4	10.1
1.1	16.2	3.0	1.2	2.2
19.3	54.1	38.9	24.3	25.6
12.6	78.4	43.9	13.0	18.9
2.1	50.0	11.7	1.8	4.4
1.9	52.8	17.3	2.1	7.5
1.5	47.2	7.1	0.6	1.3
6.3	66.7	27.4	5.9	10.6
13.3	83.3	36.0	9.8	15.9
3.2	69.4	24.4	3.9	6.6
2.3	66.7	26.4	3.3	7.5
14.7	80.6	37.6	10.1	19.8
8.8	56.8	34.3	15.4	16.3
3.3	2.6	4.0	2.9	3.9

TABLE 7 *continued*

	Total sample (N=1,856)	Public university (N=114)	Public 4-year college (N=255)
Off-campus reactions			
*"Mainly critical" reaction to activities on campus in May from:**			
Trustees	17.3	32.7	21.4
Alumni	20.1	42.3	22.6
Parents	16.9	39.4	17.3
Local citizens	30.2	50.0	36.9
State legislators	20.6	51.9	33.3
Local press	13.1	35.6	15.5
Effect on academic standards			
Perceived "detrimental" impact, on academic standards–spring 1970*	32.1	38.5	34.5
"Detrimental" impact– 1970-71 academic year*	15.3	18.5	11.9
"Beneficial" impact on instructional programs*	23.9	20.4	23.2
Student political campaign work			
More than 5% of students engaged in summer political work	11.4	20.2	10.2
Campaign recess (e.g., "Princeton Plan") Yes	3.1	4.4	2.0
Possibly	10.2	8.8	6.7

*Percentages are of the "affected colleges.

institutions and generally experienced substantially less protest than the universities or independent colleges. Ranged below the national "norm" were the Catholic institutions, the Protestant colleges, and the public two-year colleges, in that order, with the relatively high shutdown rate in the public two-year colleges occurring partly because governors of some states (as in California) asked or ordered all public institutions to close down.

Public 2-year college (N=477)	Indep. university (N=37)	Indep. 4-year college (N=198)	Prot. institution (N=338)	Catholic institution (N=227)
18.3	25.0	12.4	7.9	16.0
8.2	47.2	20.9	7.3	27.2
13.9	19.4	15.7	7.9	16.8
32.2	33.3	29.4	20.3	24.0
25.5	11.1	15.7	7.3	8.0
10.1	19.4	13.7	6.2	9.6
24.0	47.2	43.1	27.7	21.6
12.6	25.7	25.0	11.9	12.8
22.8	20.0	23.7	27.3	23.2
4.4	35.1	28.3	10.7	8.8
1.1	18.9	7.1	3.6	1.8
6.3	29.7	17.7	10.1	14.1

On the matter of "reconstituting" courses to reflect antiwar interests, there was little difference between the independent and public universities; some such efforts were reported in more than half of the universities of either type. Much less in the way of course reconstitution, ranging from a 39 percent rate in the independent four-year colleges, down to 19 percent in the public two-year colleges occurred in the other types. The pattern held for faculty modification of grading procedures, with rates ranging from 78 percent in the independent universities and 55 percent in the public universities, down to 13 percent at the Protestant institutions and two-year colleges.[4]

In regard to deviation from normal examination and grading procedures by academic division, the independent universities stood *well* apart from the field—usually by a factor of two over the public universities, and a factor of 10 to 25 over the Protestant institutions. Again the expected pattern held.

The *range* of "modification rates" across institutional types also varied among academic fields; in the professional fields, the range was in the high .40's (for example, 50 percent of the independent university business schools reportedly made some such changes, as against 2 percent of the business departments at the Protestant and two-year institutions); in the fine arts and "hard" science departments, the range was in the .60's; in the social sciences and humanities, more than 70 percentage points separated the independent universities and the Protestant institutions.

More than half (57 percent) of the presidents of independent universities said they took public stands as individuals against the Cambodia invasion or the Indochina war in general. More than one-third (34 percent) of the independent college presidents and one-fourth (28 percent) of the public university heads did so, with the figure ranging down to 9 percent among junior college presidents. With regard to institutions taking anti-Cambodia stands *as institutions*, the data for the seven types seem rather anomalous. The absolute number of colleges taking such a stance was small, and the range across the seven types is accordingly fairly small—from 6 percent in the public four-year colleges to 1 percent of the public universities.

In analyzing critical reactions from off-campus constituent groups, only those campuses that were affected by the events of the spring are considered; thus, for example, the 32.7 percent figure for public university trustees means that 33 percent of the 104 university presidents who reported (on question 8) an impact on campus operations in May said that their trustees (or regents, or whatever) were "mainly critical" of activities on campus. And it was the public universities that were most widely criticized—because the public institutions are the business of almost everyone, and also because of the relatively high incidence of violence on these campuses. Only from alumni of the independent

---

[4]The total sample "norm" is for content changes (28 percent) to be slightly more frequent than changes in grading procedures (24 percent). It is interesting that while this pattern obtained for the public and sectarian institutions (especially pronounced in the Protestant category), in the independent sector it was the grading procedures that were more often altered. Does this mean that in the independent colleges flexibility and shifting among grading systems is the norm, or does it mean that rigid systems were widely departed from?

universities was the criticism rate higher (and the independent university presidents considered their alumni to have been more critical than any other constituency). For the five types other than the public and independent universities, local citizens were seen to be most disapproving. State legislators were critical of the public institutions, especially the universities, and much less so, for obvious reasons, of the private colleges. Trustees, alumni, and parents of students at the Protestant colleges were by far the least critical of their institutions; "criticism rates" for these groups, for example, were half those for the corresponding Catholic college constituencies.

Presidents of public and independent universities and independent four-year colleges voiced the greatest concern about deteriorated academic standards in the late spring as normal academic routines for many people were altered or discontinued; these institutions experienced the most intense reactions in May, and also have traditionally maintained the highest academic standards. In all seven categories of institutions, however, at least one in five presidents expressed concern about deteriorated standards. About half of these concerned presidents, fairly uniformly across the types of institutions, believed that the impaired standards would persist into the following academic year.

The pattern of perceived "beneficial impact on instructional programs" is different, though not unexpectedly so. While the differences among the types were not large, the trend was for presidents at colleges that underwent relatively peaceful or "moderate" reactions (not *no* reaction) to view what happened as having positive consequences for the quality of teaching and learning on their campuses. These institutions—the sectarian institutions and the public two- and four-year colleges—have been less touched in recent years by student activism and broad social and political currents,[5] and the presidents of a good number of them may have welcomed the occasion for students and staff to become deeply involved in a movement that might give new meanings to instructional routines that, perhaps, have not changed significantly in many years.

The presidents' estimates of the extent of student involvement in summer political campaign work varied considerably by type of college, with the pattern of activity following closely that of previously mentioned plans made in May for such work. A third of the independent university presidents (35 percent), a fourth of the independent college presidents (28 percent), and a fifth of the public university chief executives (20 percent) indicated that 5 percent or more of their student bodies were so involved. Eleven percent or fewer of the presidents at

---

[5] Obviously there are exceptions; San Francisco State College and San Fernando Valley State College in California are only two.

the other four types of institutions reported this level of summer political work. (In addition to other student characteristics that would be associated with political activism, students enrolled at the independent colleges and universities would more often be financially able to take time in the summer to do political work.)

Both independent colleges and independent universities were more interested in the idea of a fall campaign recess. Indeed, a majority of the institutions mentioned in the ACE (1970b) summary fall into these two categories, despite the fact that the independent institutions account for only one-fourth of the population of colleges and universities.

In sum, the aftermath of the Cambodian incursion and the Kent and Jackson State killings was by no means the same at public, independent, and church-related colleges, nor was it the same at universities, four-year colleges, and two-year colleges. These different segments of American higher education tend to have different kinds of programs, cultures, and traditions; accordingly, they attract different kinds of people—students and faculty—to their doors.

The seven types of colleges considered here differ markedly in size and selectivity, as the information at the beginning of the table makes clear. Both factors are related to campus unrest. The role of institutional size is considered next.

IN INSTITUTIONS OF DIFFERENT SIZE
National surveys in previous years uniformly showed student protest to be a more common occurrence at larger rather than smaller colleges.[6] That the spring 1970 tumult was more widespread and intense at the larger schools was found in studies of the Urban Research Corporation (1970b) and Urban Institute (Buchanan & Brackett, 1970) as well as this one.

Two theories are frequently invoked to explain the relation between student activism and institutional size.[7] According to the *impersonality* theory, because of the large scale by which instructional and other operations are carried on in the multiversity, many students have no sense that the institution is concerned about them as individuals, no sense of personal worth in the university context, no sense of connectedness or loyalty to the institution. They resort to social and political activism in order to make an impact on social institutions and give meaning to their lives.

The *critical mass* theory, mentioned previously and entertained more

[6] Bayer & Astin (1969), Hodgkinson (1970), Long & Foster (1970), Peterson (1966, 1968a), Urban Research Corporation (1970a).

[7] Both have been recently discussed by Astin and Bayer (in press) and Keniston and Lerner (1971).

recently, holds more simply that the larger the student body, the greater the likelihood of there being a sufficient number (a critical mass) of students wishing to initiate some—almost any—activity, from forming a debating team to kidnapping the trustees. Only some 20 or so committed activists would be needed, for example, to plan and lead a raid on the ROTC building. Other things being equal (selectivity, regional location, etc.), the larger the student body, the greater the probability that there will be 20 such people on hand.

To analyze the May outbreak in relation to institutional size, the sample of 1,856 colleges was divided into four enrollment categories[8] which we will refer to as "small" (less than 1,000), "medium" (1,000 to 5,000), "large" (5,000 to 12,000), and "very large" (more than 12,000). Responses to the 19 selected items for the four groups are summarized in Table 8. In the mechanics of presentation and interpretation of data, Table 8 parallels Table 7 (and Tables 10 and 11).

Two-thirds of the very large institutions are Ph.D.-granting universities—replete (frequently) with graduate students, ROTC units, defense research, and so forth. Eighty-six percent of the very large, compared to 24 percent of the small, are public institutions. The very large institutions as a group are reportedly somewhat more selective than the other three, though not markedly so. The very large institutions are disproportionately in the Pacific states, especially, and in the Midwest; the Northeast, where, as we will see, students tend to be relatively "protest-prone," and the Southeast, where the opposite holds, are both underrepresented among the very large institutions.

For every action involving students or faculty (the numbers of which define the four categories) there are unbroken progressions in the data. Without exception each kind of action or method of expression was least often reported at the small colleges and most often reported at the very large institutions. As shown in Figure 1, the progressions are nearly linear for the general question about "significant impact" and for the more "moderate" modes of protest expression—peaceful demonstrations, communication with local residents, and faculty "reconstitution" activities. For the more extreme actions—strikes and destructive demonstrations—the incidence rises dramatically from the large to the very large institutions.

These results are satisfactorily explained by the "critical mass" concept. The protest actions in question were triggered at all the colleges by the same set of events which were external to the campus—the Cambodia invasion and the killings on the two campuses. At the larger institutions in the country there were sufficient numbers of students and faculty concerned enough ("protest-prone" in Keniston's words) to

[8]On the basis of answers to survey question 5 (see Appendix).

TABLE 8 Cambodia/Kent reaction profiles for institutions grouped according to size of enrollment

	Total sample (N=1,856)	*Less than 1,000 (N=722)*
Institutional factors		
Type, level		
Ph. D-granting university	9.6%	0.1%
Comprehensive college I: wide range of programs	7.5	1.1
Comprehensive college II: fewer programs	13.2	6.2
4-year liberal arts	25.5	36.2
Professional, specialized	8.0	15.7
Two-year	33.9	37.8
Other	2.3	2.9
Control, affiliation		
Public	48.6	23.8
Independent	20.0	25.9
Catholic	12.2	19.4
Protestant	18.2	29.8
Other	0.8	1.1
Selectivity		
Top 10% of high school class	8.5	5.5
Top 40%	39.6	40.2
Open admissions	50.2	51.4
Regional location		
Pacific states	12.8	9.0
Mountain states	4.4	4.2
Northeast	25.2	25.5
Southeast	24.0	25.4
Midwest	33.5	36.0
Perceived impact		
"Significant impact" on campus operations (i.e., percent "affected")	57.3 (N=1,064)	41.3 (N=298)

1,000 to 5,000 (N=757)	*5,000 to 12,000* (N=231)	*More than 12,000* (N=138)
2.9%	27.3%	67.4%
8.2	22.9	11.6
20.2	18.2	1.5
27.5	0.9	0.0
4.5	0.4	0.0
34.4	29.4	18.8
2.4	0.9	0.7
55.5	79.7	86.2
19.2	11.3	8.7
9.4	4.8	2.9
15.3	2.6	0.7
0.4	1.3	0.7
11.6	6.5	10.1
36.7	40.3	50.0
50.5	52.8	39.9
12.4	19.1	25.4
3.6	7.4	5.1
27.9	20.4	15.9
25.0	22.9	14.5
31.2	30.3	39.1
60.5 (N=458)	77.5 (N=179)	89.9 (N=124)

TABLE 8 *continued*

	Total sample (N=1,856)	Less than 1,000 (N=722)
Student-initiated actions		
Peaceful demonstrations	44.4	27.8
Communication with local area residents	40.3	28.8
Special seminars, workshops, projects, etc.	37.2	25.6
Planning for electioneering	23.1	15.1
Shutdown, one day or longer (all reasons)	20.2	14.1
General student/staff strike, day or longer	13.6	10.1
Destructive demonstration	3.9	0.4
Modification of instruction		
Some courses modified to reflect antiwar interests	27.9	19.4
Some faculty modified grading procedures	23.8	13.4
"Substantial" or "some" departure from normal exam/grading procedures, by academic field:		
Business	6.1	1.7
Education	8.9	3.2
Engineering	4.0	0.7
Fine arts	14.5	7.5
Humanities	20.2	9.7
Life sciences	10.6	5.5
Physical sciences	10.6	5.0
Social sciences	21.3	10.0
Anti-Cambodia incursion positions taken		
Stand by the president, as an individual	17.5	11.2
Institutional stand against the Cambodia invasion	3.9	3.8

1,000 to 5,000 (N=757)	5,000 to 12,000 (N=231)	More than 12,000 (N=138)
47.8	67.1	74.6
41.9	54.1	68.8
38.8	51.1	66.7
23.1	32.9	48.6
18.8	28.1	46.4
13.2	17.3	29.0
1.9	6.5	29.7
28.4	39.8	51.5
23.9	35.5	57.2
5.7	10.9	24.3
7.8	15.7	33.1
3.8	7.4	16.9
13.3	24.8	41.9
20.4	33.5	52.2
9.8	18.7	29.4
10.6	17.8	28.7
21.7	36.1	53.7
18.9	27.7	26.8
3.6	4.7	4.9

TABLE 8 *continued*

	Total sample (N=1,856)	Less than 1,000 (N=722)
Off-campus reactions		
*"Mainly critical" reaction to activities on campus in May from:**		
Trustees	17.3	8.7
Alumni	20.1	12.4
Parents	16.9	11.1
Local citizens	30.2	20.5
State legislators	20.6	9.4
Local press	13.1	6.7
Effect on academic standards		
*Perceived "detrimental" impact, on academic standards–spring 1970**	32.1	25.8
*"Detrimental" impact–1970-71 academic year**	15.3	12.4
*"Beneficial" impact on instructional programs**	23.9	30.2
Student political campaign work		
More than 5% of students engaged in summer political work	11.4	9.7
Campaign recess (e.g., "Princeton Plan")		
Yes	3.1	2.4
Possibly	10.2	9.1

*Percentages are of the "affected" colleges.

initiate a reaction; at the smaller schools there tended not to be sufficient numbers of sufficiently aroused people.

To the general "critical mass" proposition may be added an "extremes" corollary, which, rather simply, says: extreme actions will occur more often at extremely large institutions.

On matters to which "critical mass" (or "impersonality") notions are not relevant, the survey showed a slight tendency for presidents of larger institutions to have taken stands as individuals against the Cambodian incursion or the Indochina war in general. Heads of large institutions, compared to smaller ones, must either (or both) be more opposed to the war, or have felt that taking a stand would help to defuse

1,000 to 5,000 (N=757)	5,000 to 12,000 (N=231)	More than 12,000 (N=138)
14.4	25.1	36.3
16.4	25.7	43.6
13.1	19.6	40.3
28.4	36.3	50.0
17.5	27.9	47.6
10.7	17.9	29.8
33.6	31.3	42.7
16.0	14.0	20.5
23.0	20.2	17.2
12.3	11.7	15.2
3.0	3.9	6.5
11.0	11.7	9.4

potentially explosive situations (staged, albeit, by critical masses of activists). *Institutional* stands against the war, however, were not related to institutional size.

Criticism from the off-campus constituent groups consistently varied directly with campus size. Local citizens were most often seen as critical at all size levels; the local press was uniformly least often regarded as critical.

One-quarter or more of the presidents at all four size levels believed that academic standards at their institutions were impaired in the spring of 1970. A relatively large percentage (42 percent) of the heads of the very large (and typically somewhat more selective) campuses expressed

FIGURE 1 Reactions to Cambodia/Kent, by institutional size

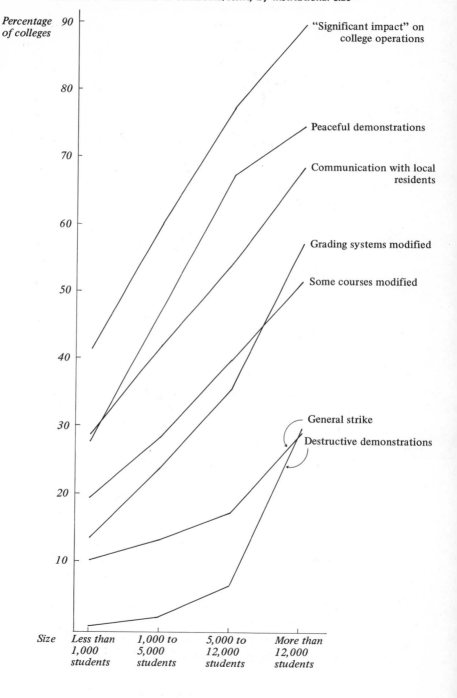

this apprehension. Again, the "rate" of concern about impaired standards during the ensuing year was roughly half that of the spring 1970 "rate" in all four size categories.

With regard to perceived "beneficial impact on instructional programs," the familiar pattern is reversed; almost one-third (30 percent) of the presidents of small colleges saw benefits to teaching and learning on their campuses; 17 percent of the heads of very large institutions so reported. Table 9 gives for each size category the rank order and percentage distribution of the four most frequent kinds of reasons presidents gave to support their judgment that the impacts on instructional programs were "beneficial."

Presidents of small colleges emphasized that a new awareness of national and international problems would improve teaching and learning. This theme was much less often mentioned by the heads of larger institutions, where the Vietnam war, overreaction of law enforcement

TABLE 9   Reasons given for regarding the campus response to Cambodia/Kent as beneficial to instructional programs, by institutional size

Question: "In your judgment, did the Cambodia/Kent/Jackson events have a positive or beneficial impact on the instructional program on your campus? If [answered] yes, please elaborate."

	Less than 1,000		*1,000 to 5,000*		*5,000 to 12,000*		*More than 12,000*	
	R*	*Percent†*	*R*	*Percent*	*R*	*Percent*	*R*	*Percent*
Increased student/staff concern about curricular change, e.g., toward greater "relevancy"	3	20.8%	1	31.3%	1	33.3%	1	33.3%
Increased student/ faculty/administrator cooperation, communication, mutual understanding	2	25.7	2	23.7	3	21.4	2½	25.0
Increased student concern about national and international problems	1	28.7	3	22.1	4	16.7	4	4.2
Increased student concern for and understanding of educational problems‡	4	19.8	4	20.6	2	26.2	2½	25.0

*Rank

†Percentage of answers given by presidents in the size category

‡These four categories of answers comprised 96 percent of all the responses given, accounting for, in the order listed above, 28 percent, 24 percent, 22 percent, and 21 percent of all the answers given by the 253 presidents who perceived "beneficial impact."

forces, and the like would have been sources of student protest for some time. Chief administrators at the larger institutions who saw benefits to the instructional program from the spring turmoil emphasized heightened student and faculty interest in curriculum reform and other educational problems.

There was only a slight (positive) relationship between presidents' perceptions of student summer political work and institutional size. And there was little relationship between college size and plans for a fall election recess (the absolute number of colleges intending to recess was very small—58 in the sample).

The factor of institutional size, of large masses of people (students and faculty) in close proximity, is critical to understanding the broad sweep of college student unrest, including the outbreak of the spring of 1970. It is important to understand, though, that students enrolled at large institutions are not on the average appreciably more activist, radical, or "protest-prone" than students attending smaller colleges (excepting, probably, those at sectarian and vocationally oriented schools).[9] The multiversity campus, however, usually contains enough (a "critical mass" of) protest-prone youths, so that when issues, such as the Cambodian invasion, come along a good bit can be made of them.

. . . BY
INSTITUTIONAL
SELECTIVITY

Another common understanding about the American college student protest movement is that active protesters are usually "brighter" than other students. This was the conclusion of, among others, Flacks (1970), Katz (1967), Keniston (1967), and Keniston and Lerner (1971) after reviews of a number of early studies of groups of protesters, usually at single institutions (often Berkeley).

More recent studies, however, reach different conclusions. Thus Kerpelman (1969) found no difference in tested (verbal) "intelligence" between left-, middle-, and right-activists at one university, but found that the combined activist groups scored higher on the intelligence test than a nonactivist group similarly comprised of these three ideological subgroups. In later studies of Berkeley left-activists and random nonactivists, Watts and Whittaker found no difference in course grades (1966) and a very small (statistically insignificant) difference in tested verbal intelligence (1969).

It is likely that differences in tested "intelligence" or course marks between radicals or activists and their more silent counterparts on campus are negligible at most colleges. The fact that most institutions with appreciable numbers of radical activists select most of their students from narrow ranges of intellectual ability would make for insig-

---

[9] On the basis of their computations, Keniston and Lerner (1971) concluded that there are *fewer* protests per 10,000 students at large institutions than at small ones.

nificant differences in intelligence among almost any set of campus subgroups. The contention that radical activists are "brighter" probably has to be based on something other than studies of students on single campuses.

If by "bright" we mean academic ability—the ability to earn high marks in school, high school, let's say, and to score high on the kinds of academic aptitude tests required for admission to college—an excellent basis for conclusions about "brightness" and activism may come from examining the incidence of protest across a range of institutions that vary in selectivity. "Selectivity" is used here to mean a policy either of (1) admitting freshmen and transfer students who meet some designated standard of demonstrated intellectual competence, or (2) from the available applicant pool, admitting those with the highest demonstrated academic ability (the best grades or test scores).

If the present survey sample is at all representative, very close to one-half of the nation's colleges are essentially *nonselective*, meaning that they admit most applicants without regard for previous academic achievement or tested aptitude.[10] The majority of these institutions are public two-year community colleges; a few are state universities that accept any graduate of the state's high schools; some were established for and are essentially open to youths of particular religious, social, and ethnic backgrounds.

Within the selective half of the total spectrum, of course, there is great variability from one college to another in the average intellectual ability of student bodies. At the top are those private (usually independent) universities and liberal arts colleges that occupy positions of great prestige and selective advantage, together with those public universities—California, for example—which, according to state master plan, operate with high minimum admissions standards. Numbering on the order of 150 (including branch campuses), these *very selective* institutions attract and admit the academic "cream" of the nation's youth.

Some 1,100 to 1,200 colleges may be regarded as *moderately selective*. Each of these institutions attempts to enroll the "best" students it can from the applicant pool it is able to muster. For the most part, applicants are from the top half of high school classes. At a good many public colleges and universities, especially in states with junior colleges, "moderate" selectivity is according to plan.

The average score on the College Board's S.A.T. for students at the very selective, moderately selective, and nonselective institutions probably would be in the high 600's, mid 500's, and low 400's respectively. This crude trichotomy, of course, belies the real range: average S.A.T.'s

---

[10]Table 7, left-hand column, third item.

at Cal Tech are close to 750; elsewhere they might easily be barely above chance scores.[11]

Previous surveys (e.g., Bayer & Astin, 1969) as well as the present one demonstrate unmistakably that campus activism is associated with intellectual ability of student body. A recent survey of undergraduates[12] indicates, however, not only that relatively larger proportions of students attending selective institutions have participated in demonstrations, but also that students at these colleges more often regard themselves as liberal or left, critical of prevailing political practices and cultural patterns, not formalistically religious, not concerned about economic security, and so forth. These are the attitudes and styles that define the value system of the "youth culture" so aptly portrayed in the *Report of the President's Commission on Campus Unrest* (President's Commission, 1970).

I would suggest that intellectual ability, substantially laid down by genetic factors as it seems to be, is basic to the eventual assumption of radical and "oppositional" values. *Obviously*, not all "bright" youths become committed to oppositional values. Those who eventually do would have been influenced early by liberal and economically secure (or insecure) parents, later by high school peer cultures of budding radicals, and then in college by radicalized peer and faculty cultures. ("Bright" but unpoliticized youths recruited from the hinterlands to the selective colleges will often also find these college norms irresistable.) All this said, however (and much more could be said, as Keniston has outlined in his book, *Young Radicals*), a fundamental principle in the radicalization process is that the more one has the intellectual capacity to understand the realities of the contemporary sociopolitical order, the more critical of it he becomes.

Whether or not the argument above has validity, the distribution of student adherents to the oppositional values of the youth culture follows substantially the pattern of admissions selectivity in American colleges and universities, and this circumstance goes far to explain the very large differences in the reaction to the events of the spring of 1970 that are set forth in Table 10.

The 1,030 four-year institutions[13] in the sample were divided into

[11]S.A.T. Verbal and Mathematical scores each range from 200 to 800.

[12]Conducted in 1969 under the auspices of the Carnegie Commission with a sample of 60,000 undergraduates.

[13]The analysis by institutional selectivity presented here is based on four-year colleges and universities only. Two-year and various professional and specialized institutions are omitted; their students are strongly vocationally oriented and hence less given to protest, and they would fall disproportionately in the open admissions category. The column of total sample results is omitted from Table 10; containing two-year institutions as they do, the total sample data would not be directly comparable to the data in the three selectivity categories.

TABLE 10 Cambodia/Kent reaction profiles for four-year colleges and universities grouped according to degree of selectivity

	Open admissions (N=297)	Top 40 percent (N=598)	Top 10 percent (N=135)	"Federal-grant" university (N=49)
Institutional factors				
Type, level				
Ph.D.-granting university	13.5	16.2	30.4	100.0
Comprehensive college I: wide range of programs	12.8	15.6	5.9	0.0
Comprehensive college II: fewer programs	33.0	21.7	10.4	0.0
4-year liberal arts	40.7	46.5	53.3	0.0
Professional, specialized	0.0	0.0	0.0	0.0
Two-year	0.0	0.0	0.0	0.0
Other	0.0	0.0	0.0	0.0
Control, affiliation				
Public	50.2	33.3	14.8	65.3
Independent	13.5	19.6	56.3	30.6
Catholic	14.8	21.1	8.9	0.0
Protestant	21.2	25.4	17.1	0.0
Other	0.3	0.3	2.2	2.0
Enrollment				
Less than 1,000	35.7	30.3	19.3	2.0
1,000 to 5,000	37.0	42.1	59.3	4.1
5,000 to 12,000	17.5	15.6	11.1	20.4
More than 12,000	9.8	11.5	9.6	73.5
Regional location				
Pacific states	6.4	9.4	14.8	14.3
Mountain states	8.8	2.8	1.5	8.2
Northeast	11.1	28.6	44.4	20.4
Southeast	30.0	23.9	19.3	24.5
Midwest	43.8	35.1	20.0	32.7
Perceived impact				
"Significant impact" on campus operations (i.e., percent "affected")	54.6 (N=162)	72.6 (N=434)	88.9 (N=120)	95.9 (N=47)

TABLE 10 *continued*

	Open admissions (N=297)	Top 40 percent (N=598)	Top 10 percent (N=135)	"Federal-grant" university (N=49)
Student-initiated actions				
Peaceful demonstrations	41.1	57.5	78.5	83.7
Communication with local area residents	33.3	52.5	80.0	83.7
Special seminars, work-shops, projects, etc.	28.0	50.0	71.9	81.6
Planning for electioneering	15.5	31.1	63.0	59.2
Shutdown, one day or longer (all reasons)	13.8	22.4	44.4	42.9
General student/staff strike, day or longer	9.1	15.9	34.8	32.7
Destructive demonstrations	5.4	6.4	8.9	30.6
Modification of instruction				
Some courses modified to reflect antiwar interests	23.2	38.5	49.6	61.2
Some faculty modified grading procedures	18.5	32.8	56.3	69.4
"Substantial" or "some" departure from normal exam/grading procedures, by academic field:				
Business	7.1	7.9	20.2	31.3
Education	9.1	14.6	25.4	43.8
Engineering	3.7	4.7	14.9	29.2
Fine arts	13.1	21.5	38.8	56.3
Humanities	16.5	28.4	48.5	66.7
Life sciences	11.1	14.8	34.3	47.9
Physical sciences	10.8	15.0	36.6	47.9
Social sciences	16.8	30.9	48.5	66.7
Anti-Cambodia incursion positions taken				
By the president, as an individual	12.8	21.7	51.9	40.8
Institutional stand against the Cambodia invasion	4.0	4.6	2.2	6.0

TABLE 10 *continued*

	Open ad-missions (N=297)	Top 40 percent (N=598)	Top 10 percent (N=135)	"Federal-grant" university (N=49)
Off-campus reactions				
"Mainly critical" reaction to activities on campus in May from: *				
Trustees	16.1	17.7	23.2	38.3
Alumni	21.0	24.4	32.5	51.1
Parents	14.8	19.6	21.7	40.4
Local citizens	25.3	33.0	39.2	53.2
State legislators	23.5	21.2	25.8	48.9
Local press	13.0	15.0	21.7	36.2
Effect on academic standards				
Perceived "detrimental" impact on academic stand-ards–spring 1970 *	23.5	32.7	51.7	42.6
"Detrimental" impact– 1970-71 academic year *	10.5	15.1	31.1	23.9
"Beneficial" impact on instructional programs *	21.6	23.7	27.7	17.4
Student political campaign work				
More than 5% of students engaged in summer political work	10.4	13.4	39.3	30.6
Campaign recess (e.g., "Princeton Plan")				
Yes	1.7	2.7	12.6	14.3
Possibly	9.8	12.9	20.0	12.2

*Percentages are of the "affected" colleges.

three selectivity categories, referred to as "very selective," "moderately selective," and "open admissions," according to whether each president indicated his entering freshmen to be "mostly from the top 10 percent of high school class(es)," "mostly from the top 40 percent," or that admission at this institution is "essentially open" (questionnaire item 3).

In the farthest right column in the table is a tabulation for what have been called "federal-grant universities" (Kerr, 1963). These are universities that receive very heavy financial support from the federal government, primarily for scientific research. For purposes of this study, they are 49 of the 50 universities that received the most federal money—$14,000,000 or more—during the 1968-1969 academic year (see questionnaire item 4).[14] They would be the nation's most renowned institutions of higher education.

One sees at the top of the table that the "very selective" institutions are disproportionately Ph.D.-granting universities and liberal arts colleges, with comprehensive four-year colleges correspondingly underrepresented. More than half of the 135 very selective institutions are independent in control; only 15 percent are public, as compared to 33 percent for the moderately selective colleges and 50 percent for open-admission colleges. Selectivity varies consistently in each geographical region; Northeastern and Pacific states, for example, together account for 59 percent, 38 percent, and 18 percent of the very selective, moderately selective, and open-admission (four-year) colleges. Average size of the institutions in the three categories, however, is quite similar; proportions of very large institutions (enrollment over 12,000) in each category are almost exactly the same. Critical mass notions will not help in interpreting the substantive data in the table.

That the May turmoil was much more intense at the more selective colleges may be read in the steeply ascending progressions of data for the various kinds of essentially student actions in Table 10. Almost twice as many very selective colleges experienced some form of peaceful demonstration as did open-admission colleges. Planning for election campaign work got underway at four times as many of the very selective institutions. Four times as many of the most selective colleges reported student/staff strikes. And so forth.

The notable exception to this general pattern was in the use of violence. Compared to the more peaceful actions, the increase in destructive actions across the three categories was quite small. It would be important to understand. Are critical masses of extremists generally not prevalent at selective institutions? Are "brighter" students somehow more "responsible," better able to remain non-violent during demonstrations, etc.? Were the responses of administrative and faculty leaders somehow more appropriate at the selective college?[15]

---

[14]The "federal-grant" category is not independent of the three selectivity groups. Sixteen of the 49 (33 percent) are in the "very selective" category, 26 (53 percent) are "moderately selective," and seven (14 percent) have open admissions.

[15]Outside law enforcement forces, for example, were brought onto 3 percent of the very selective campuses during May, and onto 7 percent of the moderately selective and 3 percent of the open-admission campuses (despite the generally higher level of activity at the most selective colleges).

Modification of course content and grading procedures by faculty increased substantially with institutional selectivity, with the curious reversal of the content and grading deviations (mentioned in footnote 4, Chapter 4) recurring in the sample of very selective institutions. "Reconstitution rates" for the various academic divisions, as depicted in Figure 2, uniformly increased in the expected manner. For natural sciences, business, and engineering faculties, the increase was particularly striking between the moderately selective and the very selective colleges.

Critical mass theory would not explain these trends; the size of the various departments or divisions would on the average not be larger in the more selective institutions (in the professional fields they may well be smaller). Instead, we suggest that the propositions made earlier about intellectual ability and oppositional values in students could apply also to faculty in the selective colleges. They could also apply to their presidents, over half of whom (52 percent) in the very selective group took public stands as individuals against the Cambodian invasion.

Concern about deteriorated academic standards in the wake of the upheaval was registered by close to one in four (24 percent) of the presidents of the "affected" open-admission colleges; by one in three (33 percent) of the moderately selective college presidents; and by one in two (52 percent) presidents of very selective institutions. This last figure, predictably, represents the highest level of concern about standards of any subgroup of institutions considered in the study; in the aggregate, the academic standards of these "very selective" institutions would be the highest in the country.

Paradoxically, the trend was for the presidents of the more selective colleges to more often perceive a "beneficial impact on instructional programs" from Cambodia/Kent. The differences (ranging from 22 percent to 28 percent) were not large, and the kinds of reasons for seeing benefits given by the three groups of presidents were not notably different.

Student involvement in summer political campaign work—ordinarily for congressional peace candidates—was more prevalent, by a very large margin, among students from the very selective institutions.[16] Likewise, November election recesses were proportionately much more common at the very selective colleges (indeed the idea was conceived at Princeton University). "Bright" (and affluent) students, some would say the nation's "best," then, sought in disproportionate numbers to

[16]Representing only 7 percent of the total sample of 1,856 institutions, the 135 very selective four-year colleges contributed 25 percent (53 out of 212) of all the institutions from which 5 percent or more of the students reportedly engaged in summer political work.

FIGURE 2 Modification of examination and grading procedures in eight academic fields, by institutional selectivity

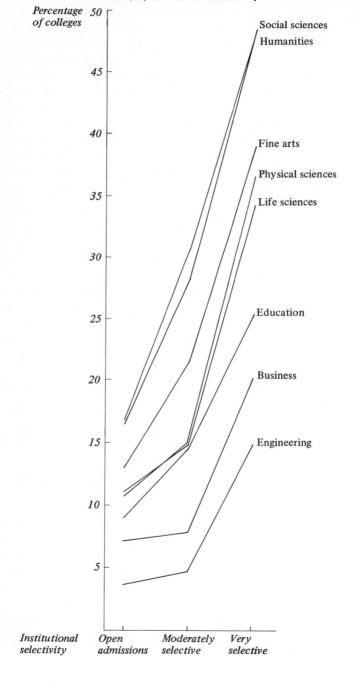

realize their antiwar sentiments through establishment politics, to make conventional political processes work in behalf of somewhat radical goals.

The 49 "federal-grant universities" in the sample occupy a central position in the national higher education system, and indeed in the nation as a whole. They are meccas for the nation's most gifted students and scholars. Their graduate schools are counted on heavily for research and development, and for training scientific and intellectual manpower. Their professional schools prepare the nation's civic and governmental leaders. Such considerations give the fact that the country's "great universities" have undergone the most serious disruption up to and including the spring of 1970 special significance.

As Table 10 shows, almost three-quarters of the sample of universities are very large (enrollment over 12,000), and they tend to be fairly selective (footnote 14, Chapter 4).[17] Thus in the "typical" federal-grant university, both the "critical mass" and the selectivity principles would be operative; bright people committed to oppositional values would be there, and they would be there in large numbers (large enough to include unstable freaks and potential bombers, as well as "due-process radicals"). These campuses would usually also have ready targets in the form of ROTC buildings, applied physics labs, and such. Often there are other people in neighboring street and drop-out communities eager to join in the action.

At any rate, the (arid, disembodied) figures in the right hand column of Table 10 indicate truly frenzied activity, which on nearly one-third (31 percent) of these campuses escalated into violence. Outside law enforcement forces were brought onto one-third (35 percent) of these 49 campuses.

Some of the faculty at well over half the "federal-grant" universities supported "no business as usual" responses by modifying their courses. Reflecting the high incidence of violence, critical reactions from all the off-campus constituent groups were more frequently reported by presidents of these institutions than by any other group of presidents in the study.

... BY GEOGRAPHICAL REGION
While the differences in the scope of the campus reaction to Cambodia/Kent in various regions of the country were not as large as those by institutional type, level, size and selectivity, they were substantial nonetheless. "Significant impact" on campus operations was reported at three-quarters (76 percent) of the colleges in the Northeast, by two-thirds (68 percent) of the institutions in the Pacific states, by roughly half of those in the Midwestern (51 percent) and Mountain states (52

[17]Two-thirds are public; almost one-third are independent.

percent), and by 41 percent of the colleges in the Southeastern states.

The regional pattern of protest reported here is generally consistent with the results of earlier national studies, as well as with the other surveys of protest in the spring of 1970. Thus in the academic years 1964-65 and 1967-68, organized protest over "off-campus" issues (the Vietnam war and related issues, and civil rights) was most frequent in the Northeastern and Far Western states (similar rates), least frequent in Southern colleges, with the heartland falling in between (Peterson, 1966, 1968a). The Urban Institute and Urban Research Corporation surveys of post-May 1 protest used identical regional breakdowns and obtained remarkably similar results: protest was most frequent in the East and least frequent in the South; the West (17 states) and Midwest fell in between, separated by the narrowest of margins (the West higher by 2 to 3 percentage points).

An adequate explanation for the regional variation set forth in Table 11 will be somewhat less simple, certainly less parsimonious, than those advanced regarding institutional size, selectivity, and so forth. A few clues are found in the information at the top of Table 11. In the South there are relatively many Protestant colleges (many would be Baptist of varying degrees of fundamentalism), at which student and faculty activism has been minimal. The Mountain states in the sample have disproportionate numbers of open-admission institutions, which are also usually characterized by campus peace. Institutions in the Pacific states are larger on the average, a factor associated with campus conflict; on the other hand, though, there are many (usually quiescent) two-year colleges in California. In the Northeast, an important part of the story lies in the selectivity figures and the large number of independent colleges and universities (these two factors go together, as indicated in Tables 7 and 10).

But the more important reasons for this geographical variation in "protest-proneness" of students and campus activism, however, are rooted in social, economic, ethnic, and religious traditions and conditions in the several regions. Growing out of the interaction of these demographic factors are the characteristic political values of the regions that have been so consistently delineated by public opinion polls and studies of political self-identification ("liberal," "conservative," etc.), party preference, and voting behavior. The general pattern, needless to say, is for people in the East (the Northeast, more precisely) to be the most liberal, people in the South (blacks excepted) to be the most conservative, with the rest of the country falling in between. Liberal political climates would presumably offer the least resistance to the kinds of subcultures that nourish development and expression of oppositional values.

Regional variation in political ideology and activism of college freshmen is documented annually by ACE's Office of Research. Thus, for example, among freshmen entering in 1969, the proportions reporting having "demonstrated for a change in some military policy" during their senior year in high school were 8.2 percent, 7.0 percent, 5.8 percent, and 4.4 percent for entrants to colleges in the East, West, Midwest, and South, respectively (Creager, *et al.*, 1969). The regions also vary in the number of institutions located in large urban centers— the focal points for many of the nation's imperfections, and the site of most of its contemporary radical movements. Students attending colleges in the Southeast and Mountain states (of our Table 11 breakdown), for example, would be relatively less influenced by these currents.

In Table 11, one sees that the incidence of "peaceful demonstrations"—a catchall of familiar modes of expressing concern—paralleled the responses to the general question about "significant impact on college operations." The three kinds of activities listed next—communication with local residents, special projects, etc., and planning for electioneering—were in some sense out-of-the-ordinary, more creative, and demanding of a greater degree of commitment, and here the largest gap was between the rest of the country and the Far Western and Northeastern colleges; in part, the relatively high rates for the latter two could be explained by the critical-mass and selectivity principles respectively. The same pattern held for the stronger actions—shutdowns and strikes—for presumably some of the same reasons, although the high shutdown rate in the Pacific states may to a large degree be attributed to Governor Reagan's request that California's institutions close down, and the high "strike" rate in the Northeast could reflect wide use in that region of the word "strike," owing to the presence of a "National Strike Center" at Brandeis University (outside Boston), to describe what was taking place on these campuses. These caveats notwithstanding, we can make the generalization that—with the exception of the use of violence—the stronger or more extreme the actions, the larger the regional differences (for "peaceful demonstrations," colleges in the Southeast and the Northeast differed by a factor of two; for "general student/staff strikes," these two regions differed by a factor of almost nine). While the incidence of violence tended to follow the usual regional pattern (low in the South, etc.), the actual differences were negligible; as we saw earlier, violence tended to occur in large public universities, which know no regional boundaries.

Course content and grading changes show steady increases from the Southeast to the Northeast. When specific academic fields are considered, however, the significant break in the progressions is between the Northeast and the rest of the country; cores of relatively radical faculty in engineering, education, business, and the natural sciences, for

TABLE 11 Cambodia/Kent reaction profiles for institutions classified by geographical region

	Total sample (N=1,856)	*South-east (N=445)*
Institutional factors		
Type, level		
Ph.D.-granting university	9.6	9.2
Comprehensive college I: wide range of programs	7.5	9.0
Comprehensive college II: fewer programs	13.2	13.0
4-year liberal arts	25.5	26.7
Professional, specialized	8.0	4.7
Two-year	33.9	33.3
Other	2.3	4.0
Control, affiliation		
Public	48.6	52.1
Independent	20.0	12.6
Catholic	12.2	7.6
Protestant	18.2	27.0
Other	0.8	0.7
Selectivity		
Top 10% of high school class	8.5	6.3
Top 40%	39.6	37.8
Open admissions	50.2	54.8
Total enrollment		
Less than 1,000	38.9	41.1
1,000 to 5,000	40.8	42.5
5,000 to 12,000	12.5	11.9
More than 12,000	7.4	4.5
Perceived impact		
"Significant impact" on campus operations (i.e., percent "affected")	57.3 (N=1,064)	41.4 (N=184)

Mountain states (N=82)	Midwest (N=621)	Pacific states (N=238)	North-east (N=468)
18.3	9.8	8.0	9.2
6.1	7.1	8.4	6.4
9.8	12.4	13.0	14.7
20.7	29.8	11.3	26.7
4.9	7.3	9.2	12.0
40.2	31.7	49.6	28.6
0.0	1.9	0.4	2.4
73.2	47.5	63.5	34.6
11.0	13.5	15.1	39.5
4.9	14.8	6.7	17.3
8.5	23.2	14.3	7.1
2.4	0.5	0.4	1.3
4.9	5.0	9.2	15.6
23.2	39.9	26.5	50.4
70.7	54.4	61.3	31.0
36.6	41.9	27.3	39.3
32.9	38.0	39.5	45.1
20.7	11.3	18.5	10.0
8.5	8.7	14.7	4.7
52.4 (N=43)	51.1 (N=317)	67.7 (N=161)	76.3 (N=357)

TABLE 11 *continued*

	Total sample (N=1,856)	South-east (N=445)
Student-initiated actions		
Peaceful demonstrations	44.4	29.2
Communication with local area residents	40.3	20.5
Special seminars, workshops, projects, etc.	37.2	30.0
Planning for electioneering	23.1	11.2
Shutdown, one day or longer (all reasons)	20.2	7.4
General student/staff strike, day or longer	13.6	3.4
Destructive demonstrations	3.9	2.5
Modification of instruction		
Some courses modified to reflect antiwar interests	27.9	13.7
Some faculty modified grading procedures	23.8	10.6
"Substantial" or "some" departure from normal exam/grading procedures, by academic field:		
Business	6.1	4.3
Education	8.9	4.7
Engineering	4.0	2.0
Fine arts	14.5	8.1
Humanities	20.2	11.0
Life sciences	10.6	6.3
Physical sciences	10.6	6.3
Social sciences	21.3	11.0
Anti-Cambodia incursion positions taken		
By the president, as an individual	17.5	7.9
Institutional stand against the Cambodia invasion	3.9	1.6

Mountain states (N=82)	Midwest (N=621)	Pacific states (N=238)	North-east (N=468)
39.0	39.1	54.2	61.5
30.5	34.0	55.9	61.3
29.3	30.0	47.1	59.6
15.9	17.7	32.8	37.6
7.3	11.8	38.7	36.3
6.1	8.2	18.5	29.5
3.7	4.5	4.6	4.3
20.7	25.9	34.0	42.3
12.2	15.9	29.0	45.9
2.4	3.4	3.0	13.7
6.1	5.6	5.9	18.9
2.4	1.9	3.4	9.2
11.0	9.5	13.6	28.3
13.4	12.9	23.7	38.0
8.5	6.4	6.8	22.5
8.5	5.5	5.1	24.7
14.6	14.2	26.7	38.8
7.3	13.0	23.5	31.4
0.0	2.6	2.9	9.1

TABLE 11 *continued*

	Total sample (N=1,856)	South-east (N=445)
Off-campus reactions		
*"Mainly critical" reaction to activities on campus in May from:**		
Trustees	17.3	13.6
Alumni	20.1	13.0
Parents	16.9	13.0
Local citizens	30.2	24.5
State legislators	20.6	14.7
Local press	13.1	12.5
Effect on academic standards		
Perceived "detrimental" impact on academic standards–spring 1970*	32.1	23.4
"Detrimental" impact–1970-71 academic year*	15.3	13.1
"Beneficial" impact on instructional programs*	23.9	20.8
Student campaign work		
More than 5% of students engaged in summer political work	11.4	8.8
Campaign recess (e.g., "Princeton Plan")		
Yes	3.1	0.2
Possibly	10.2	7.6

*Percentages are of the "affected" colleges.

example, manage to subsist in Northeastern colleges to a degree unparalleled elsewhere in the country.

Presidential opposition to the Cambodian invasion tended to follow the regional pattern of student and faculty opposition; less than 8 percent of the presidents in the Southeastern and Mountain states took public stands, as compared to 31 percent in the Northeast.[18] As regards

[18]It may have occurred to some readers that presidents who are personally opposed to the Indochina war may have been inclined to report greater opposition on campus to the Cambodia incursion than in fact existed. Indeed, that beliefs (motivations, at the least) color perceptions is a psychological truism. Some evidence that such a "response set" is *not* seriously distorting the survey is implicit in the data for the academic divisions in the Pacific states; relatively high rates of "no business-as-usual" were reported for only three of the eight academic fields by presidents who were relatively opposed to the Cambodian actions.

Mountain states (N=82)	Midwest (N=621)	Pacific states (N=238)	North-east (N=468)
25.6	14.2	25.5	17.4
32.6	18.6	13.7	26.6
20.9	14.5	19.3	19.6
32.6	29.7	29.8	33.3
32.6	20.2	26.1	20.2
14.0	10.1	17.4	14.0
16.3	27.4	29.2	44.0
7.0	13.9	14.5	18.9
23.3	22.7	28.9	24.5
13.4	9.3	13.5	15.2
1.2	2.7	1.3	7.7
9.8	7.4	10.9	16.2

institutional stands, while the absolute numbers were small, the regional variation was even more striking. Of all the colleges in the sample that reportedly took "institutional stands," 60 percent (44 out of the 74) were in the Northeast.

The regional variation in the extent of criticism from off-campus groups is difficult to summarize. Generally the differences were small, reflecting mainly the small differences in the incidence of violence. "Criticism rates," with the exception of criticism by the press, were lowest in the Southeast where the level of protest was the lowest. Interestingly, the highest off-campus criticism rates were reported by presidents in the Mountain states (where the level of activity was *also* quite low)[19]; disproportionate numbers of the institutions in that

[19] Criticism from the press was most often reported in the Pacific states.

region are public, and the resolute people (taxpayers) of the Mountain states may be somewhat less than tolerant of youthful troublemakers, faultfinding intellectuals, and so forth.[20]

Presidential perceptions of negative impact on academic standards followed the pattern of selectivity across the regions; differences were substantial, ranging from 16 percent in the Mountain states to 44 percent of the presidents of Northeastern colleges voicing concern about impaired standards. Variation in judged "beneficial impact on instructional programs" was negligible.

In contrast to the sizable regional variation in plans made in May for student political campaign work, the differences across the regions in reported summer work were quite small. While the rates were still the highest by narrow margins in the Northeast and Pacific states (where antiwar candidates tended to be most available), the decline from the earlier levels of enthusiasm are impressive in these two regions. Fall campaign recesses were scheduled by many more colleges in the Northeast than elsewhere; of the 58 colleges in the total sample anticipating recesses, 36 were in the Northeast.

IN SUMMARY   Respectful of the diversity in functions, purposes, and traditions among the more than 2,500 colleges and universities in the land, the purpose in this chapter has been to show how the reaction to the Cambodia invasion and the Kent and Jackson State shootings was systematically related to several of the dimensions that define this diversity. The nature and scope of the reaction in diverse classes of colleges were described in some detail, and several propositions that may help to explain the patterns of protest observed were set forth.

We saw, first, in regard to type of control and degree level, that the independent and public universities experienced the strongest upheaval and that the reaction was mildest at the Catholic and Protestant institutions and in the two-year colleges. The very general assertion was made that different kinds of students (and faculty) in terms of values and backgrounds are characteristically attracted to each of the different types of institutions—universities, four-year colleges, and junior colleges, and those that are public, independent, and church-related.

Next, the striking differences in the intensity of the May turmoil at institutions of different size were documented, and I advanced the rather simple notion of a "critical mass"[21] to explain these differences (including the pattern of violence). Similarly, large differences in the

---

[20] Because the number of presidents reporting is small, only 43 ("affected" colleges), all the data for the Mountain states region are somewhat less reliable than the other data in the table.

[21] The larger the institution, the greater the likelihood of there being "critical masses" of students on hand ready to engage in any kind of activity.

scope of the reaction (excepting violence) occurred at colleges differing in degree of selectivity, and in this regard the general assertion about "different kinds of students" (and faculty) was refined to focus on what I called "oppositional values," for the acquisition of which, it was suggested, some level of intellectual ability is critically necessary. Finally, we found patterns of reaction to be more pronounced in the Northeast and less pronounced in the South, in comparison to other regions of the country. These data were briefly discussed in terms of broad social and political climates that would be expected to give rise to varying degrees of support for or resistance to oppositional subcultures.

If nothing else, the material in this chapter should serve as an antidote to easy conclusions about "what happened" in the spring of 1970. On a limited number of campuses—perhaps 100—the response rapidly escalated into excesses, violence, and near-paralysis of the institution. At many more colleges the response was peaceful, resourceful, and but briefly disruptive of the normal work of the institution. And at some 1,100 out of all the colleges (43 percent of the sample), the Cambodia invasion and the Kent and Jackson State killings made no appreciable impact at all.

5. Consequences for the College: Presidents' Views

The last question in the survey asked each president whose college had been affected by Cambodia/Kent/Jackson to write out what he (she) considered to be the single most significant long-run implication of the events of the spring of 1970 for his campus. A wide range of answers was given. Attempts to reduce the responses to a relatively small (e.g., eight or ten) general categories all seemed to do a disservice to the genuine variety in the answers. The 26 categories into which the answers were eventually coded are listed in Table 12, ranked according to the frequency with which each kind of implication was mentioned. The N is the number of answers (presidents) in each category; the *percent* is the corresponding percentage of the 1,064 presidents of "affected" colleges.

TABLE 12 Presidents' beliefs about the consequences for their campuses of Cambodia and Kent State (N=1,064)

Question: "What do you consider to be the single *most significant* long-run implication of the events of the spring of 1970 for your campus?"

	Theme	N	Percent
1)	Increased student/staff active concern about national and international problems.	167	15.7
2)	Increased cooperation and mutual trust among students, faculty, and administrators.	138	13.0
3)	Likelihood of continued violence, increased alienation from established authority, etc.	70	6.7
4)	Increased polarization between and within campus groups.	67	6.3
5)	The institution will not be able to remain neutral or detached in relation to social problems.	63	5.9
6)	Increased student reliance on "moderate" tactics, working within the system, etc.	62	5.8
7)	Increased active student concern with college affairs and educational problems.	55	5.2
8)	Increased college receptivity to institutional reform.	51	4.8

	Theme	*N*	*Percent*
9)	Backlash from the public, loss of public or alumni support, etc.	51	4.7
10)	Decreased institutional receptivity to change, stronger controls on student and faculty activists, etc.	50	4.7
11)	Greater awareness/concern among faculty of college affairs/issues/problems.	38	3.6
12)	Likelihood/concern that the campus may/will become politicized; campus will become a staging ground for radical or partisan political action, possibility of political indoctrination in the classroom, etc.	29	2.7
13)	Awareness that institutional neutrality is an issue and that questions of institutional stance on social problems will have to be faced.	24	2.3
14)	Greater involvement/activism on the part of moderates (students/faculty).	24	2.3
15)	Greater student influence in campus affairs.	23	2.2
16)	Necessity for the institution to enforce strict neutrality in relation to social issues (e.g., social action projects, political clubs, etc., may have to be moved off campus).	19	1.8
17)	Increased shared decision making (involving students, faculty, administrators, trustees).	18	1.7
18)	Decline in general quality of education; academic standards may deteriorate, students/faculty may become less committed to intellectual activities, etc.	16	1.5
19)	Students developing greater confidence/competence/skill in bringing about change at the college.	16	1.5
20)	Declining influence of radicals (students, faculty).	12	1.1
21)	Improved relations with the public, increased public support, etc.	10	.9
22)	Academic freedom will be reduced, undermined, etc.	10	.9
23)	Students developing greater confidence/competence/skill to bring about change in the society.	10	.9
24)	General quality of education will improve, intellectual climate will become more stimulating, etc.	10	.9
25)	Students capable of greater responsibility (than previously assumed).	8	.8
26)	Decreased violence, intimidation, etc. in the future.	4	.4
	No response	19	1.8

What the reader makes of the distribution of responses in Table 12 will depend on his educational and political values. (My own thoughts on these perceived implications are for the most saved for the concluding chapter). It does seem noteworthy that more presidents stressed essentially positive or constructive consequences than stressed negative ones. Most people, I think, would agree that entries 3, 4, 9, 10, 12, 18, and 22 are clearly undesirable consequences; together they account for (only) about one-fourth (28 percent) of all the presidents' answers. Presidents' beliefs about long-run implications, however, are by no means uniform across different types of colleges. One rather easy generalization, we will see, is that the heads of large and prestigious universities are more negative and more apprehensive than their counterparts at smaller and lesser-known colleges, which is not surprising in view of the greater turmoil at the universities in May.

Table 13 presents a summary of the most frequently mentioned implications, with the data organized according to each of the four classifications set forth in the previous chapter (control/level, size, selectivity, and geographical region). For each breakdown, the five "themes" that were noted most frequently by the presidents are indicated. Each entry consists of a number followed by a percentage (in parentheses); the number designates the theme (from the list in Table 12), and the percentage is of the "affected" colleges in each type. For example, for the theme most frequently cited by the chief administrators at the public universities, the entry is 9 (18.3); the number 9 designates "backlash from the public, etc.," and this theme was mentioned by 18.3 percent of the heads of the (104) "affected" public universities. More than one number accompanied by one percentage figure indicates a tie—that two or more themes were mentioned by the same number of presidents in the category.

BY CONTROL/LEVEL OF INSTITUTION

As suggested, the presidents at the kinds of institutions that have undergone the most disruption, in the spring of 1970 and previously, were more pessimistic than other presidents about long-term prospects. Heads of public universities were particularly concerned about loss of public confidence, polarization on campus, and the likelihood that institutional policies would become more rigid (signified, perhaps, by calls for "guidelines" on this or that matter). Presidents of independent universities were chiefly concerned about even greater levels of student alienation and violence in the months ahead, and about the inability of their institutions to remain politically neutral. At other types of institutions, where overt conflict has been less frequent, the presidents more often foresaw, as a result of Cambodia/Kent, greater active concern of student and staff for broad national and international problems and issues. Almost one in four (24 percent) of the presidents of Catholic colleges affected by the events of the spring singled out this theme. Consistently ranking second in frequency in all but the public and independent universities was the theme of improved communication and trust among students, faculty, and administrators.

TABLE 13[a] Presidents' view of consequences of Cambodia/Kent, by control/level, size, selectivity, and geographical location of college

By control/ level	Public univ. (N=104)	Public 4-year college (N=168)	Public 2-year college (N=208)	Indep. univ. (N=36)
Most freq. cited	9(18.3)	1(13.7)	1(14.4)	3,5 (11.1)
2nd most freq. cited	4(10.6)	2(13.1)	2(13.0)	1,6,8 10 (8.3)
3rd most freq. cited	10 (9.6)	3,4 (10.1)	7 (7.2)	
4th most freq. cited	2,3,8 13 (6.7)	7,10 (8.3)	3,4 (5.3)	
5th most freq. cited	5,6 (5.8)	9 (7.1)	8 (4.8)	

By size	Less than 1,000 (N=298)	1,000 to 5,000 (N=458)	5,000 to 12,000 (N=179)	More than 12,000 (N=124)
Most freq. cited	1(23.2)	1(15.5)	2(12.3)	9(12.1)
2nd most freq. cited	2(16.1)	2(12.7)	1 (9.5)	1,2,3,4 10 (8.1)
3rd most freq. cited	5,6 (7.4)	3 (7.4)	3 (8.4)	5 (7.3)
4th most freq. cited	4,7 (4.4)	4 (6.6)	9 (7.8)	8,13 (5.6)
5th most freq. cited	8 (4.0)	7 (6.1)	4 (7.3)	7 (4.8)

By selectivity	Open admissions (N=162)	Top 40 percent (N=434)	Top 10 percent (N=120)	"Federal grant" (N=47)
Most freq. cited	1(16.7)	1(15.7)	2(13.3)	9(19.1)
2nd most freq. cited	2(13.0)	2(11.8)	1(12.5)	4(12.8)
3rd most freq. cited	3 (9.3)	4 (7.4)	5(10.8)	3(10.6)
4th most freq. cited	10 (8.6)	3,5 (6.2)	3 (9.2)	5,13 (8.5)
5th most freq. cited	4,8 (6.8)	9 (6.0)	9 (8.3)	2,10,12 (6.4)

Indep. 4-year college (N=153)	*Prot. Insti- tution* (N=177)	*Cath. Insti- tution* (N=125)	*Total sample* (N=1,064)
1(15.7)	1(19.8)	1(24.0)	1(15.7)
2(14.4)	2(15.8)	2(11.2)	2(13.0)
5(10.5)	5 (8.5)	4 (6.4)	3 (6.6)
3 (7.8)	6 (7.3)	8 (5.6)	4 (6.3)
6,8 (5.9)	8 (5.6)	5,7,14 (4.0)	5 (5.9)

Total sample (N=1,064)			
1(15.7)			
2(13.0)			
3 (6.6)			
4 (6.3)			
5 (5.9)			

TABLE 13[a] *continued*

By geo-graphical location	Southeast (N=184)	Mountain states (N=43)	Midwest (N=317)	Pacific states (N=161)
Most freq. cited	1(16.8)	2,8(11.6)	1(17.4)	1,2(14.3)
2nd most freq. cited	2(14.7)	10 (9.3)	2(12.3)	9 (8.7)
3rd most freq. cited	6 (8.7)	3,6,7 9,11 (7.0)	5 (7.3)	4,10 (7.5)
4th most freq. cited	3 (7.1)		3 (6.9)	5,7,12 (5.0)
5th most freq. cited	4,5 (6.5)		6,7 (5.7)	6 (4.3)

[a]See text, page 73, for explanation of entries.

BY SIZE OF INSTITUTION Beliefs about long-run implications of the May turbulence for the college also differed for presidents of institutions of different size. Theme 1, "greater student/staff concern about national and international problems," was mentioned by about one-fourth (23 percent) of the small college presidents. Theme 1 together with theme 2, improved student/faculty/administrator trust, accounted for 39 percent of all the small college presidents' answers; they accounted for 28 percent, 22 percent, and 16 percent of the answers from the medium, large, and very large institutions respectively. Theme 6, "increased student use of 'moderate' tactics," appears (only) in the small college rankings (where extremism has been minimal), and, conversely, for these colleges, theme 3, "increased alienation and violence," does not appear. Theme 9, "loss of public support," is first mentioned by presidents of the large institutions, and is the consequence *most* often anticipated by the heads of the very large institutions, most of which are public universities. Finally, the prospect of greater institutional rigidity (theme 10) was raised (ranked) only by presidents of the very large institutions, reflecting, as suggested earlier, strong negative reactions from trustees and other off-campus constituencies against the extensive strike and course-reconstitution activities that took place on these campuses.

BY SELECTIVITY When the presidents were grouped according to institutional selectivity, there were surprisingly few differences in their beliefs about long-run implications of Cambodia/Kent for their campuses. Presidents of very selective institutions seemed somewhat more optimistic about the future of their colleges *as communities*; theme 2, "increased mutual

Northeast	Total sample
(N=357)	*(N=1,064)*
1(15.7)	1(15.7)
2(12.3)	2(13.0)
4 (7.6)	3 (6.6)
3 (7.3)	4 (6.3)
5 (5.3)	5 (5.9)

trust," was mentioned most frequently, while theme 4, "increased polarization," dropped out of the ranking altogether.

FEDERAL GRANT UNIVERSITIES Quite significant, however, were the impressions of the presidents of "federal grant" universities about the consequences of the turmoil for the welfare of their institutions. Chief executives of these eminent universities were almost entirely negative. Nine of the 47 presidents (19 percent) spoke of a "backlash from the public" and "loss of public support" (theme 9); no doubt these were heads of public universities. Six (13 percent) mentioned "increased polarization" on the campus (theme 4). Five anticipated "increased alienation and violence" at their institutions (theme 3). Four presidents voiced concern about maintaining institutional neutrality (theme 5),[1] and five more expected that their institutions would be forced to confront questions of neutrality versus advocacy (theme 13). Three anticipated new rigidities and repressive policies (theme 10), and three more indicated that there were prospects of outright politicization (theme 12).

Granted, the sample of 47 is small, and the interpretations, recorded during the summer of 1970, were personal, temporal, and not necessarily the most valid that could be placed on events. Nonetheless, in the aggregate they stand as a measure of the contemporary pessimism verging on despair of the leaders of those institutions from which the academic community and the nation have come to expect the most, and which have been torn by the bitterest strife.

[1] One can, of course, raise questions about the meaning of "institutional neutrality" at a university receiving several millions of dollars from government sources.

BY GEOGRAPHICAL
REGION

Finally, there seemed to be few consistent or meaningful regional patterns in the presidents' beliefs about longer-run impacts of the spring protests. Themes 1 and 2 accounted for from 32 to 23 percent of the responses in every locality except the Mountain states. Of the (relatively few) presidents in the Mountain states, some foresaw an improved climate for change on their campuses (theme 8), while others anticipated greater institutional rigidities (theme 10). Southern college presidents were perhaps the most positive in their outlooks, with the theme (6), "greater reliance on moderate tactics," entering their rankings. Prospects for a backlash from the public (theme 9) were seen slightly more often by the heads of Pacific coast institutions, who also were relatively mindful of the likelihood of new institutional rigidities.

6. Notes on Meanings

My intent to this point has been to describe the campus reaction to Cambodia and Kent State (as it was understood by the presidents of the nation's colleges) in as reasonable and even-handed way as I could. The bulk of the survey data has been given in tabular form, and readers may browse therein, determine for themselves what is important, and draw their own meanings and conclusions. What follows, however, is a more or less explicit statement of what, in my opinion, are the main lessons of the upheaval of May 1970.

ACADEMIC
NORMALCY
ABANDONED

For great numbers of American college students, including many of the most intellectually gifted, there is no firm commitment to academic work as it is presently carried on. In May 1970, hundreds of thousands of people on the campuses proved capable, with remarkable swiftness, of turning away from their usual academic work, totally or in some degree, and focusing their energies on other activities.

Some course modification—involving only one or two courses in some places, scores of courses at others—occurred at roughly one-fourth of the nation's colleges. Some number of classes were *cancelled* at one in four colleges. Normal instructional activities shut down entirely for a day or longer at one-fifth—over 500—of the colleges. Such were measures of the flight from academic business-as-usual in May of 1970.

Furthermore, it was where the academic ship was seemingly most secure—at the most prestigious independent and "federal grant" universities, homes of the "best" students and faculty—that it was abandoned the fastest. And as between liberal arts and professional "ships" it was the former that was more readily abandoned. Some may be quick, for a variety of reasons, to pronounce liberal arts education bankrupt; probably more important is the fact that the liberal arts divisions attract most of academe's radical leaders and activists, for whom school work is almost always secondary. All in all, May 1970 saw an unprecedented refusal of the campus community to carry on with academic work per usual, and an important lesson must surely be that conventional academic activities in these times, especially in the liberal arts, command no unyielding allegiance, and that the values that supposedly undergird academic life are fragile indeed.

THE UPRISING UNSUSTAINED
American mass student political movements, as phenomena involving continuing participation in collective actions by many more than the theretofore highly committed activists, are unable to sustain themselves in the absence of new or continuing issues or provocations. The May protest began to fade by mid-month; the relative calm on the campuses the following fall astonished almost all observers.

It may seem inconsistent to stress the ease with which customary routines are relinquished and a mass reaction set into motion on the one hand, and the surprising demise of the movement and the return to seeming normalcy on the other. Yet one may appreciate how really volatile contemporary youth and students are; massive turmoil in May to massive calm in September. The campus scene is mercurial indeed. The writing was probably on the wall early in the summer when very few presidents reported either efforts to keep "reconstitution" on their campuses alive or any significant number of students involved in congressional campaign work.

Outlined below are some probable reasons why the uprising, the "reconstitution," of the spring failed to carry into the fall. The various factors would have operated in different combinations in different individuals on different campuses, and would be among the reasons why almost any mass student movement in America has been unable to sustain itself.

Personal priorities Renewed concern about academic or professional careers which were jeopardized by the May political activities; involvement in (or return to) new usually nonpolitical life styles—communal living, satisfying and therapeutic human relations, Eastern religion, traveling and camping, organic foods, groovy clothes, drugs, music, crafts, "neo-fundamentalist Christianity," good loving and sex, athletics, karate, and so forth.

Sense of futility Cynicism about the unresponsiveness of institutions; disillusionment with conventional politics; absence of national leaders with whom to identify; frustration with tactics (nothing works, and one can get hurt); pessimism about ever changing the system; a tiredness from trying; generalized bitterness; despair.

The seasonal cycle Summer: away from campus comrades, interaction with different kinds of people, new perspectives on past events. Fall: time for a fresh start, academic work seems new and interesting, many activist leaders from the previous spring have not returned, political groups not yet organized. Winter: a transitional time. Spring: academic boredom has replaced academic interest, new protest leadership has emerged, political groups have gotten together, warm sunny days facilitate mass gatherings and lowered inhibitions.

The "morning after" experience Feelings among some students and faculty of the essential wrongness of the politicized university, of the inappropriateness of hyper-emotionalism in the university, of having been manipulated by charismatic leaders.

Other movements, causes Women's liberation, gay liberation, jock liberation; Soviet Jewry and the Jewish Defense League; ecology; making one's commune work.

Repression—real or imagined Movements against established authority inevitably beget counter actions: college "crackdowns" on rule breakers; May protest leaders expelled or involved in civil court trials; college guidelines for "appropriate conduct" developed; state laws passed to ensure campus order.[1]

Improved campus climate Modest academic reforms in effect in the fall making for greater freedom and flexibility within the curriculum; better relations between students and faculty; new, more participatory campus governance arrangements (all these improved conditions despite new efforts, mentioned above, to prevent radical excesses).

National and international events American troops out of Cambodia on schedule, casualty rates low, war seemingly winding down; draft reforms; national elections inconclusive from students' standpoint, President conciliatory, Vice-President muted.

EDUCATIONAL CLIMATES CHANGED *Educational reform trends toward more student options and more personalized learning experiences, underway for some time, were greatly accelerated by the May upheaval. In particular, many people in their academic work will be seeking to keep alive, if not the structure or the political content of the May uprising, the spirit of those days, the satisfaction from doing meaningful things in meaningful ways, together.*

[1] According to the Educational Commission of the States, bills and resolutions to prevent campus disorders were adopted in 32 states during 1969 and 1970.

Twelve percent of the presidents reported that specific changes, additions, etc., in either academic programs or campus governance arrangements had been instituted by mid-summer as the result of Cambodia/Kent/Jackson. Some 15 percent indicated that planning for reforms or new programs was underway, again as a result of the May upheaval. However, it appears that such structural changes as were made, such as a (single) new course in "community political analysis" in one college's political science department, were relatively minor. Furthermore, no instance is known where an institution which was more or less politicized in May ("reorganized to oppose the war") was in operation in the fall similarly politicized.

Instead, what *was* carried over on many campuses was the memory of how good it felt doing new things, personally important things, in new ways. People got a feel for what education *could* be like. Professors, especially, became aware of new possibilities for teaching and learning. Almost one in four presidents (23 percent) said that the May reaction had led to "greater unity" between faculty and students.[2] Not all students (and professors), of course, will want to recapture the "spirit of May" in their studies. Many will, however, and the result will be new pressures for "relevant" learning experiences, integrating thought and action (as Bilorusky points out), closer student/faculty relations, non-competitive or no grading, opportunities for collective rather than individual projects, and so forth—all of which are part of an undergraduate educational reform movement that has been continuing for the past five years or so.

(A possible danger on some campuses is that the new spirit will run up against new pressures for retrenchment from campus authorities, the latter a not unexpected result of increased public criticism and prevailing college financial difficulties. Such are the seeds of further, harsher confrontations.)

CAMPUS
OPPOSITION
TO THE
NATIONAL
GOVERNMENT
WIDENED

Cambodia and Kent State had the effect of extending the opposition on the nation's campuses to the national government and its foreign and domestic policies. Thousands of normally apathetic students and staff became "educated" and concerned. Distrust of the Administration reached new heights.

The long-run implication of the events of the spring noted most frequently by the presidents in the survey, it will be recalled, had to do with increased student and staff concern about national and international issues, problems, and conditions. Explicit or implicit in most

[2]Nine percent said "greater division"; the rest indicated "no significant impact" on student/faculty relations.

of these comments, and they came most notably from presidents of campuses not known as centers of protest, was the idea of increased criticism on campus of the war and national priorities. The theme mentioned third most frequently explicitly anticipated greater levels of conflict and violence. Various surveys of student opinion—a Harris Poll in May 1970 (discussed in the Scranton Report), a Gallup Poll taken in December 1970—point to a seemingly dramatic spread of oppositional values since the Cambodia invasion.[3] Indeed, one suspects that if the USA found it necessary to fight an all-out war, it would be difficult to raise a full-scale army (in view of the present level of noncooperation with the selective service system).

Campus opposition to the government has focused chiefly on the White House and the Pentagon, although Congress and the legislative process have not escaped. The level of antagonism and mistrust in the academic community directed at the government was stressed to the President in July 1970 by his campus advisors Alexander Heard and James Cheek. That the President, in making campus appearances, has had to pick his colleges carefully is well-known.

It has become commonplace to speak of gaps, divisions, and polarizations in American society. Surely the gap between a large segment of the academic world and the national government is one of the most serious. It has been growing since the assasination of John F. Kennedy; it was deepened dramatically by the events of the spring and the campaign rhetoric of the summer and fall of 1970. Thus, in the spring of 1971 we find large elements of the "counter culture" or "adversary culture" on the campuses polarized in opposition to the state and its supporters in "loyal" America, seemingly waiting for some provocation that will ignite the conflict anew.

PUBLIC
SUPPORT
OF THE
UNIVERSITY
ERODED

Public confidence in and support for the colleges and universities, declining in the past several years in the aftermath of campus conflict, dropped further as a result of the May uprising. Public antagonism is especially strong toward universities experiencing violence in May 1970, and before. In consequence, financial resources have become restricted for individual institutions and state systems, and prospects for needed federal financial aid grow dim.

Attitudinal support from the public slips away when tax-supported higher education institutions seem unable to maintain internal order, when students engage in activities and life styles unrelated to familiar understandings of student behavior, when institutions seemingly

---

[3] For example, 44 percent of students in the Gallup Poll answered affirmatively to the question "Do you think violence is sometimes justified to bring about change in American society, or not?" (as compared to 14 percent of the general public).

become organized to work toward achievement of some political program (as happened, in part, in May). Not all colleges are objects of public outrage in equal manner (although all, in the longer run, are likely to suffer some of the consequences of a disenchanted public). In particular, the public universities and the so-called "federal-grant universities" (recipients of large sums of public money for research) were the institutions that in recent years have experienced the most violent confrontations, and it was their presidents who most often stressed loss of public support as the major consequence for their campus of the May upheaval. In fact, one lesson from the survey data seems to be that the public will tolerate a large measure of dissent and "non-conformism" on the campus, but not coercive disruption and violence.

Public displeasure, fanned by campaign rhetoric, probably reached its peak at the time of the November elections. It was manifested, before and after November, in a stream of state laws designed to promote campus peace, as well as in calls from many university boards of trustees for guidelines spelling out appropriate conduct on the campus. Representatives of the public (or a large segment of it) scorned administrators for their permissiveness, faculty for dereliction of duty (politicians became more than usually interested in faculty salary levels, teaching loads, tenure, and so forth), and students for their extremism and lack of appreciation for what they have been given.

The chief weapon in the "crackdown" is the power of the purse, which many state governments and some community college districts are wielding with considerable effect.[4] No salary increases, no new staff or programs (while enrollments continue to increase) make for much unease in faculty ranks, especially when the academic job market is tight. People on the campuses go about their normal duties tense, muttering about repression and loss of academic freedom, waiting.

Another consequence of the May turmoil and the ensuing erosion of public support is that prospects for substantial federal aid, so urgently needed by many institutions, become dimmer. Federal money for basic research in the universities has already been cut back. Proposals to make unrestricted grants to all accredited institutions are not likely to be viewed favorably by Congress. Proposals for a large-scale program of grants to needy youths (perhaps with matching grants to institutions) will be scrutinized closely; indeed, as Daniel Moynihan (1970) has pointed out, the whole movement toward universal higher education is likely to be set back.

In short, the May turmoil accelerated the decline of public confidence in many colleges and universities; worsened local town-gown rela-

[4]Campus unrest, of course, is not the only (nor perhaps even the most important) reason for the financial difficulties of many colleges and universities.

tions; reduced institutional autonomy *viz.*, statewide authorities; and probably postponed the day when large-scale federal aid to the colleges will make possible needed new programs.

IT CAN HAPPEN
AGAIN

What happened in May 1970—widespread stoppage of higher education per normal, strong protest throughout the land—can happen again. The tinder of discontent on the campus remains dry. The spark could be a calculated governmental action, or more tragically, an unintended consequence of an action, or both—as with Cambodia and Kent State. Any new outbreak could be expected to have serious consequences for both universities and society.

To say that the campuses have been relatively quiet since May 1970 is not to say that they have been pacified. The educational climate on many campuses has been improved, to be sure; academic work has been further loosened or "derigidified," and students are relatively satisfied with this aspect of their lives. But at the same time, opposition to the war and current national priorities runs deeper than ever.

The signal for any new large-scale confrontation is not likely to come from the campuses or the counter culture. The student and intellectual communities are now too pessimistic about any movement they would launch having any impact. No student-initiated antiwar program has much chance of attracting mass student support. The spark for the conflagration, if there is to be one, will most likely be a deliberate governmental policy decision—to invade North Vietnam, or to use tactical nuclear weapons, for example. Or the spark could be an unintended consequence of some other (perhaps minor) action—for example, the use of American troops to rescue the South Vietnamese in Laos or North Vietnam with much loss of life, or, closer to home, greatly expanded draft quotas, or an event similar to the Kent and Jackson State killings.

Because of the revulsion on the campuses to many policies of the national government, because of public aversion to radically politicized campuses, and because of the substantial tolerance on all sides for the use of force and violence, any new mass reaction from the campuses could escalate into a conflict that could leave both university and society in extremely serious disarray.

CAMPUS AND
SOCIETY:
SOME POSSIBLE
FUTURES

Depending in large part on events, one can imagine three possible, fairly short-run futures for higher education viz., *American society. At the worst: spiraling conflict leading to severe educational and social breakdown. At the best: reconciliation, coming with the end of the war and reordering of national priorities. Most likely: continuation of the present situation of unfriendly coexistence and sporadic confrontation.*

While it is not inconceivable that an effective political movement from the campuses could be mounted sometime in the near future, the mood now is one of futility and waiting. It seems, therefore, that future relations between campus and society will depend most critically on decisions and actions of governmental leaders.

The first possibility, a future of breakdown, would be set in motion by an event such as use of tactical nuclear weapons; the reaction from the campuses would be powerful, and there could follow ever stronger cycles of repression by the state and counter reaction from the campuses, leading eventually to civil war between "adversary" culture and "loyal" culture, and finally to the collapse of the American nation as we know it. Such a scenario may seem wildly far-fetched in these days of relative calm; it was much on the mind of quite a few people between May and November of 1970, however (*cf.*, Trow, 1970; Wicker, 1970).

For the second possibility, reconciliation, to happen, there would need to be complete disengagement from Indochina *and* the launching of major governmental programs to ameliorate social and economic conditions at home. It is not unreasonable to expect that a whole new spirit of understanding and tolerance would accompany these governmental redirections and the ensuing surge of support from the campuses.

The third possible future, continuation of the *status quo*, assumes that there will be no startling shifts in national policies and no deliberate or fortuitous events that would ignite the campuses.[5] While American involvement in the ground war in Southeast Asia may soon end, the air war seems destined to continue, and it will be some years before new national purposes are articulated and the country begins to reunite. In the meantime on the campuses there are likely to be continued attacks on ROTC, defense-related research facilities, and other symbols of university cooperation with the war effort; trashing of property as peaceful rallies get out of hand; intimidation of faculty who seem too sympathetic with the government; and so forth. Until the time of reconciliation (perhaps 1976 will be the year of the New American Revolution), it will be a matter of the university muddling through, making the best of it, avoiding the great repression that could lead to an end of the university as a functioning intellectual enterprise, or to open revolt.

MUDDLING THROUGH *Responsible college leaders in the immediate future will have little choice other than working to keep their institutions intact in the face*

[5] People who assert that campus unrest will not cease with the end of the Indochina war are probably right.

of internal campus tensions and an unfriendly external environment. A number of changes in the structure and functioning of colleges might be effective in a holding action—until a new era begins.

One could point to many measures that may help institutions to endure with minimal further loss of freedom of expression, institutional autonomy, and student and faculty support for the values of the institution—and also with minimum disruption, intimidation, and violence. Several of the baker's dozen of topics below have been touched on in other reports.[6]

Consensus on the nature of the institution Systematically undertake to reach *some* degree of internal consensus about the general nature and goals of the institution; seek understandings about basic institutional values through democratic interaction of all individuals on campus.

Institutional neutrality Unless there is institutional consensus to the contrary, act as though institutional neutrality were not a myth;[7] work to eliminate university sponsorship of war-related activities such as ROTC and classified research; forgo taking stands as an institution on issues of public policy; guard against political tests in evaluating faculty or students.

The academic program Expand content offerings to accommodate the educational interests and capabilities of the total student body; expand teaching, examination, and grading options within and among courses to accommodate the diversity in student learning styles; develop special learning experiences for freshmen; humanize the work of graduate students.

Faculty work Reward faculty according to the competency they bring to achieving accepted institutional goals (which on most campuses means rewarding primarily for teaching skill); employ systematic student evaluation in appraising teaching competency; encourage faculty to develop ways by which they can act en masse and with effect when accepted institutional values come under attack.

---

[6]The report of the President's Commission on Campus Unrest (1970); the report of the Special Committee on Campus Tensions established by the American Council on Education (1970a); the "First Report" of the Assembly on College Goals and Governance (AAAS, 1971). A summary of the major points in these and other relevant documents is given in the Carnegie Commission's special report, *Dissent and Disruption: Proposals for Consideration by the Campus* (1971).

[7]Which it is, some would argue, at any institution receiving government funds.

Institutional size Plan not to expand institutions presently enrolling more than 15,000 students; plan so that no new institution enrolls over 15,000; eliminate large lecture classes; consider reorganizing large institutions into subunits, in the affairs of which both students and staff can participate and otherwise come together.[8]

Governance Conceive of the campus as a community of people sharing accepted institutional values, rather than as an amalgam of competing interest groups; eliminate student government as such;[9] decentralize decision making and encourage people to participate; help people to understand how to operate within existing structures, or to change them.

Institutional capacity to respond Create mechanisms for *prompt* decision making, grievance processing, and resolution of real conflicts between real interests. Work to create a climate of flexibility on campus in which new programs to meet new needs can be readily launched and constructive accommodations (breaks from normalcy) be reached in times of crisis.

Internal communication Develop mechanisms for ensuring that people are continuously informed about campus affairs, especially in times of crisis; develop procedures so that information, ideas, and reactions can easily flow throughout the organizational structure; ensure easy accessibility to campus officials; make full-time use of communication specialists.

Student life Except where there is consensus for another policy, arrange for students to have very great freedom and responsibility to regulate their lives, within the bounds of civil law; cease managing dormitories in populated areas; turn management of student services over to students.

Minority student access Work toward the goal of enrolling minority students in roughly the proportion they exist in the institution's geographic constituency or sphere of recruitment; develop curricula and supporting services that will meet the educational needs of these new students.

[8] A clear finding from the survey was that the violence that occurred in May took place almost entirely at the very large universities.

[9] As suggested by Earl McGrath (1970).

Relating to the adjacent community Be responsive, in urban areas, to problems in the urban community: relate curricula to the urban situation; train professionals in urban work; provide technical assistance; include community representatives in planning for college actions that affect the community; maintain a stance of openness to communication with all segments of the neighboring community.

Relations with civil authorities Maintain open and cooperative relations with local law enforcement agencies: for timely detection of potential criminal acts, for coordinating actions or police on or near the campus during emergencies, for use of civil courts when civil laws are violated.

Interpreting the university to the public Assess the accomplishments of college programs; render meaningful account for the expenditure of public funds; try to continuously interpret the work and the problems of the institution to the public.

TOWARD NEW
CONCEPTIONS OF
YOUTH AND
HIGHER
EDUCATION

In a time of great cultural change, with youth in the vanguard, American higher education in its conventional forms has lost much credibility and legitimacy both on and off the campus. New national understandings of youth and higher education must soon be reached. Both the diversity of youthful interests and the over-arching goal of national reconciliation will need to be recognized. Although the search should begin now, now is not the time—because of deep divisions in the land—for promulgating such new national policies.

The ease with which students and young faculty turned to other activities in May attests to their declining commitment to customary academic work. The collective, noncompetitive, and interpersonally close patterns that the lives of many people took during May 1970 are indicative of how they would prefer to live. Indeed, the growth of uban and rural communes across the country, populated chiefly by relatively young people, hints at social changes of the greatest significance.[10] Declining job markets in many technical, scientific, and academic fields reflect changing national needs for educated manpower. These and other cultural and economic trends will require that the total system of higher education in America, after a quarter century of somewhat headlong and mindless expansion, soon accept new roles that will more explicitly serve the nation and individuals.

[10]In one poll of 8,000 college freshmen and juniors, 17 percent "favored communal living" (reported in the *Chronicle of Higher Education*, February 15, 1971).

These exigencies have not gone unrecognized. In his February 1971 message to Congress on higher education, President Nixon suggested that "1971 can be a year of national debate on the goals and potentials of our system of higher education, a time of opportunity to discover new concepts of mission and purpose." In proposing a National Foundation for Higher Education, the President noted that it "would have as its mandate a review of the overall needs of the American people for post-secondary education."

That ours is a heterogeneous, pluralistic society is a truism. That diverse kinds of postsecondary school experiences will continue to be needed is equally obvious. There will still need to be facilities for study in the humanities and arts, for scientific and technical training, professional (e.g., medical) training, literacy training. But there will have to be new opportunities—for example, for continuing education for older adults, and for advanced study in areas such as ecological analysis, urban design, legal services, and health care delivery, in which the best minds of the generation can channel their talents and ideals.

Perhaps more crucial, though, is the fact that increasing numbers of youths are choosing not to become involved in formal higher education at all. Some would be interested in meaningful public or social service. More wish to "drop out" to experiment with new ("alternate") forms of living—as in street people neighborhoods, settled communes, or mobile bands. These are the youth who find standard American life meaningless, and they include some of the most intelligent and sensitive of the generation.

How, for purposes of public policy, is "education" or "higher education" to be defined? Must it have intellectual content in some sense? Can it include public service—in the sense of students going out and helping people in need of help? Can it include personalistic and living-in-a-community objectives, as would be consistent with the kind of society some would say we are moving toward? Should these various interests of youth be met by different social institutions—for example, by colleges as places for academic learning, a national service corps, youth sanctuaries? Or can a case be made for comprehensive (higher) learning communities which integrate a diversity of youth concerns, including academic learning, artistic expression, public service, and life-style experimentation?[11]

Whatever the structural arrangements may look like, it is imperative that a national policy for youth be in the interest of national reconciliation. Which means it must accommodate all the nation's youth—the sons and duaghters of all the nation's taxpayers. No segment can be

[11] I have written elsewhere about some of the elements of such a model (Peterson, in press).

written off. A "new deal" for youth in short, must be part of the larger effort to become one nation.

Thus it most certainly is time to begin talking seriously about the shape that higher education in the future could take. But it is not the time to decide. It is unlikely that viable policies can be agreed upon until the many walls of distrust and animosity across the land begin to fall away. This, it seems, will not happen until American foreign militarism ends and real work to improve the quality of life at home begins.

The agenda is clear.

References

American Academy of Arts and Sciences: *A First Report: The Assembly on University Goals and Governance*, Cambridge, 1971.

American Council on Education: *Campus Tensions: Analysis and Recommendations*, Washington, D.C., April 1970 (1970a).

American Council on Education: "Survey Finds 21 Colleges with Recesses Scheduled," *Higher Education and National Affairs*, October 23, 1970, pp. 3-5 (1970b).

Astin, Alexander W.: "New Evidence on Campus Unrest, 1969-70," *Educational Record*, vol. 52, 1971, pp. 41-46.

Astin, Alexander W., and Alan E. Bayer: "Antecedents and Consequents of Disruptive Campus Protests," in *Measurement and Evaluation in Guidance*, in press.

Bayer, Alan E., and Alexander W. Astin: "Violence and Disruption on the U.S. Campus, 1968-69," *Educational Record*, vol. 50, 1969, pp. 337-50.

Brann, James: "The Straight Kids Lose Faith," *Change*, vol. 2, no. 6, 1970, pp. 66-71.

Buchanan, Garth, and Joan Brackett: *Survey of Campus Incidents as Interpreted by College Presidents, Faculty Chairmen and Student Body Presidents*, report submitted to the President's Commission on Campus Unrest, Urban Institute, Washington, D.C., October 1970.

Bunzel, J. H.: "Costs of the Politicized College," *Educational Record*, vol. 50, 1969, pp. 131-37.

Carnegie Commission on Higher Education: *Dissent and Disruption: Proposals for Consideration by the Campus*, McGraw-Hill Book Company, New York, 1971.

Cheek, James: quoted in Ian E. McNett: "Jackson State Shootings Stir New Wave of Unrest," *Chronicle of Higher Education*, May 25, 1970.

Chronicle of Higher Education, February 15, 1971.

Clark, Burton R., and Martin Trow: "The Organizational Context," in Theodore M. Newcomb and Everett K. Wilson (eds.), *College Peer Groups*, Aldine Publishing Company, Chicago, 1966.

Cottle, Thomas J.: "Strike Week in Chicago," *Change*, vol. 2, no. 4, 1970, pp. 19-28.

Creager, John A., *et al.: National Norms for Entering College Freshmen: Fall 1969*, American Council on Education Research Reports, vol. 4, no. 7, Washington, D.C., 1969.

DeMott, Benjamin: "Seven Days in May: The Teacher in Apocalypse," *Change*, vol. 2, no. 5, 1970, pp. 55-68.

Diamond, Stanley, and Edward Nell: "The Old School at the New School," *New York Review of Books*, June 18, 1970, pp. 38-43.

Disruptions at Loeb, Courant, and Kimball, News Bureau, New York University, New York, September 1970.

Flacks, Richard: "Who Protests: The Social Bases of the Student Movement," in Julian Foster and Durward Long (eds.), *Protest! Student Activism in America*, William Morrow and Company, New York, 1970.

Gaddy, Dale: *The Scope of Organized Student Protest in Junior Colleges*, American Association of Junior Colleges, Washington, D.C., 1970.

Gilbert Youth Research: *American Youth Attitudes*, paper prepared for the White House Conference on Children and Youth, Gilbert Marketing Group, New York, February 1970.

Hodgkinson, Harold L.: *Institutions in Transition*, Carnegie Commission on Higher Education, Berkeley, Cal., 1970.

Katz, J.: *The Student Activists: Rights, Needs, and Powers of Undergraduates*, report prepared for the Office of Education, U.S. Department of Health, Education and Welfare, Washington, D.C., 1967.

Keniston, Kenneth: "The Sources of Student Dissent," *Journal of Social Issues*, vol. 23, no. 3, 1967, pp. 108-37.

Keniston, Kenneth, and Michael Lerner: *The Unholy Alliance Against the Campus*, reprinted from *New York Times Magazine* by Carnegie Commission on Higher Education, Berkeley, Cal., 1971.

Kerpelman, Larry C.: "Student Political Activism and Ideology: Comparative Characteristics of Activists and Nonactivists," *Journal of Counseling Psychology*, vol. 16, 1969, pp. 8-13.

Kerr, Clark: *The Uses of the University*, Harper and Row, New York, 1963.

Krislov, Samuel: "The Obligation to Reject Engagement," *American Association of University Professors Bulletin*, vol. 56, 1970, pp. 276-78.

Lipset, S. M., and E. C. Ladd, Jr.: "...And What Professors Think," *Psychology Today*, vol. 4, no. 6, 1970, pp. 49-51, 106.

Long, Durward, and Julian Foster: "Levels of Protest," in Julian Foster and Durward Long (eds.), *Protest! Student Activism in America*, William Morrow and Company, New York, 1970.

McGrath, Earl J.: *Should Students Share the Power?*, Temple University Press, Philadelphia, 1970.

Michener, James A.: *Kent State: What Happened and Why*, Reader's Digest and Random House, New York (in press). Condensed version appeared in *Reader's Digest*, March and April 1971.

Moynihan, Daniel P.: *On Universal Higher Education*, paper presented at the 53rd annual meeting, American Council on Education, St. Louis, Mo., October 1970.

Newman, Frank, et al.: *Report on Higher Education*, report to the Secretary, U.S. Department of Health, Education and Welfare, Washington, D.C., March 1971.

New York Times, October 25, 1970 and December 23, 1970.

Peterson, Richard: *The Scope of Organized Student Protest in 1964-1965*, Educational Testing Service, Princeton, N.J., 1966.

Peterson, Richard: *The Scope of Organized Student Protest in 1967-68*, Educational Testing Service, Princeton, N.J., 1968a.

Peterson, Richard: "The Student Left in American Higher Education," *Daedalus*, vol. 97, no. 1, 1968b, pp. 293-317.

Peterson, Richard: "The Regional University and Comprehensive College: Some Ideas," in W. Frank Hull IV and Richard E. Perry (ed.), *An American Organization: The American University and its Administration*, Center for the Study of Higher Education, Toledo, Ohio (in press).

Peterson, R. E., J. A. Centra, R. T. Hartnett, and R. L. Linn: *Institutional Functioning Inventory; Preliminary Technical Manual*, Educational Testing Service, Princeton, N.J., 1970.

President's Commission on Campus Unrest: *Report of the President's Commission on Campus Unrest*, Washington, D.C., September 1970.

Rogers, J. M.: *Staffing American Colleges and Universities*, Office of Education, U.S. Department of Health, Education and Welfare, Washington, D.C., 1967.

Stone, I. F.: *The Killings at Kent State*, New York Review, New York, 1970.

Stone, Lawrence: "Princeton in the Nation's Service," *New York Review of Books*, June 18, 1970, pp. 7-10.

Swenson, Jack: "War Symposia at Canada," *Junior College Journal*, vol. 41, no. 2, 1970, pp. 32-34.

Trow, Martin: *Admissions and the Crisis in American Higher Education*, paper presented at the 53rd annual meeting, American Council on Education, St. Louis, Mo., October 1970.

U.S. Office of Education: *U.S. Office of Education Directory, 1967-1968*, and *1969-1970*, U.S. Department of Health, Education and Welfare, Washington, D.C., 1968 and 1970.

Urban Research Corporation: *Right on! A Documentary of Student Protest*, Bantam Books, New York, 1970a.

Urban Research Corporation: *On Strike...Shut It Down: A Report on the First National Student Strike in U.S. History*, Chicago, May 1970b.

Watts, William A., Steve Lynch, and David Whittaker: "Alienation and Activism in Today's College-age Youth: Socialization Patterns and Current Family Relationships," *Journal of Counseling Psychology*, vol. 16, 1969, pp. 1-7.

Watts, William A., and David Whittaker: "Free Speech Advocates at Berkeley," *Journal of Applied Behavioral Science*, vol. 2, 1966, pp. 41-61.

Wicker, Tom: "In the Nation: The Dead at Kent State," *New York Times*, May 7, 1970.

Widmer, Kingsley: "The End of Hired Learning?", *American Association of University Professors Bulletin*, vol. 56, 1970, pp. 273-75.

Williamson, Edward G., and John Cowan: *The American Students' Freedom of Expression*, University of Minnesota Press, Minneapolis, 1966.

Wolfe, Alan: "A Summer Look at the Spring Events," *American Association of University Professors Bulletin*, vol. 56, 1970, pp. 269-72.

Part Two

Reconstituting University and Society: Implications from the Berkeley Situation

1. Historical Context: Unfolding the Events and Experiences

In Berkeley on April 5, 1970, an audience of 500 heard Peter Scott, professor of English at the University of California, Berkeley, give a history of United States involvement in Laos. His speech was part of a Laos Day program at King Junior High School, which also included speeches by journalist Jacques de Cornoy, of *Le Monde*, and Tom Hayden, a member of the "Chicago Seven." On April 6, anthropology professor Gerald Berreman, also of Berkeley, spoke before an audience of 80 at the first of a series of student-organized anthropology seminars on the Berkeley campus. He maintained that the United States government is supporting anthropological research to facilitate counterinsurgency activities in Chile, Laos, and other countries throughout the world (From the Berkeley student newspaper, *The Daily Californian*, April 6 & 7, 1970). On May 6, Scott presented a history of American involvement in Cambodia and Southeast Asia, but this time his audience was 17,000 people at a Berkeley campuswide convocation. On May 27, Berreman spoke to 5,000 at a second campuswide convocation.

Scott's and Berreman's second speeches came, of course, after President Nixon's April 30 announcement of the United States invasion of Cambodia. The announcement set off protests on many of the nation's college campuses. Protests intensified following the killing of four students at Kent State University. Describing the protest on the Berkeley campus, Chancellor Roger Heyns said on June 18, 1970, in *Report to Regents' Committee on Educational Policy* (1970):

The power and strength of this outburst was awesome. It was a great groundswell, a tidal movement of genuine feeling and opinion on the part of most students and many faculty, expressive of real concern over the present problems and the future destiny of the United States. There has been nothing like it before in American history. It was real and it had to be heeded. No one on campus doubted this.

For several weeks prior to the United States move into Cambodia, there had been more political activity than usual around the Berkeley campus. Some students and faculty had registered people for the June primary elections; many had worked for the election of Ron Dellums, a black city councilman, to the United States Congress. The Student Mobilization Committee had sponsored a week of antiwar activities across the country, April 13-18. A group of students and faculty called Scientists and Engineers for Social and Political Action (SESPA) had demanded an end to secret and war-related research at the university. The Committee for Participant Education, which had sponsored a controversial course involving Eldridge Cleaver in the fall of 1968, offered student-initiated courses on such topics as the "New American Revolution." Some students had participated in the formation of the Berkeley Tenants' Union.

The most significant campus activism during April, however, were the sometimes violent confrontations over the on-campus status of ROTC. Although many students favored university disaffiliation with ROTC, most were disturbed by the rock-throwing tactics of a few demonstrators. As a result, only a few hundred students were substantially involved in campus antiwar activity at that time.

Then, following President Nixon's April 30 announcement of the Cambodia invasion, student sentiment changed. One student interviewed in the middle of May, for example, said: "Before the Cambodian announcement, I was bothered by the violence of the ROTC demonstrations, but I am [now] sympathetic with getting them off the campus. When I watched Nixon on television that Thursday night I felt he was not speaking the desires of the people." An editorial in *The Daily Californian* (May 1, 1970) reflected the reaction of many students, faculty, and staff:

Like masochists, many of us gathered in front of television sets last night to listen to the president. . . .
Political powerlessness and personal frustration increased a hundred times for many. We have heard all the phrases, we have watched this same TV show continually for the last six years.
The problems facing this country, that Nixon and his cohorts symbolize, are not new. They will not be solved quickly. . . .
We are all in the same predicament. The more we realize this, the sooner we will recognize our potential strength to overcome and rebuild our society. . . .

Protest built quickly at Berkeley following the President's Thursday announcement. The following Monday (May 4) an editorial called "A Time to Act" appeared in *The Daily Californian* (as well as a number of other campus newspapers around the country; 11 college newspaper editors had met following the Cambodian invasion to promote a nationwide student protest):

President Nixon's unwarranted and illegal decision to send American combat forces into Cambodia, and to resume the bombing of North Vietnam, demands militant, immediate and continued opposition from all Americans. . . .

The need for action has never been so great and so urgent. [The editorial then called for a nationwide strike of students, faculty, staff, and administrators. It stated that such a strike would be "a dramatic symbol of our opposition to a corrupt and immoral war," and that "within a society so permeated with inequality, immorality and destruction a classroom education becomes a hollow, meaningless exercise."]

But the necessity of a strike extends even far beyond these reasons. The strike is necessary to free the academic community from activities of secondary importance and to open it up to the primary task of building renewed opposition to the war. It is necessary to permit the academic community to first solidify its own opposition and then to ask immediately to extend this opposition beyond these campuses.

Many students, faculty, and staff felt a sense of urgency and the need to demonstrate their concern about the Cambodian invasion. One member of the nonacademic staff said that the invasion was seen by many as a ". . . first step toward war with China and eventual nuclear holocaust." She expressed the feeling that: "This is our last chance to have an effect on governmental policies. People feel they must get involved now because *now* is the turning point." A faculty member wrote in a letter to *The Daily Californian* (May 5, 1970):

The action of President Nixon in expanding the war in Southeast Asia is, in my judgment, an atrocity of such magnitude as to demand an articulate, immediate and militant response. . . .

I therefore urge my colleagues to consider the suspension of regular academic functions in order to demonstrate concern over the course of American foreign policy, if only for a temporary symbolic period of time.

Students and faculty in some departments began to schedule meetings to discuss the crisis and possible activities in light of the proposed strike. Students in some classes voted to go on strike, and one class went to California Hall to discuss the campus crisis with a representative of the administration. Some students began to circulate petitions asking senators to protest the President's action and to call for immediate withdrawal from Southeast Asia. Members of the Peace Brigade, a group of students committed to nonviolent social change, sent a resolution to the Berkeley City Council, condemning the war and demanding an immediate withdrawal of troops.

When news of the killings at Kent State reached the campus, most people expressed outrage and fear. At a meeting of People's Coalition, an organization of left-wing groups, some of the more militant activists exhorted the crowd of over 1,000 students and nonstudents to "trash" (damage) Callaghan Hall, the naval ROTC building. Others urged moderation, but about 300 demonstrators did later attempt to burn Callaghan Hall and the Asian Studies center (*Daily Californian*, May 5, 1970).

Meanwhile, an ad hoc Faculty-Student Peace Committee had begun to make plans for a nonviolent, campuswide protest. Previously, on Sunday night, May 3, over 150 faculty members had met and passed a resolution calling for a campuswide convocation on Wednesday—at which they would call for a strike. Acting on Monday, the Faculty Senate voted to recommend to the Chancellor ". . . a convocation to discuss and consider appropriate responses by the campus community to the grave consequences of the recent widening of the war in Southeast Asia" (U.C. Academic Senate, 1970). The Senate also recommended that from Tuesday to Friday ". . . all normal academic exercises be suspended in order to provide the University community sufficient further time in which to consider together matters of extraordinary national concern" (*Ibid*). Chancellor Heyns released a statement on Monday night approving the convocation, and announcing that he would discuss the suspension of academic activities with the deans of the schools and colleges on Tuesday.

The next day, the Faculty-Student Peace Committee stated again its position that the university should be an open forum devoted to considering the situation in Southeast Asia. The Committee said that the Cambodian invasion and the Kent State slayings ". . . prohibit and make a mockery of business as usual, especially academic business" and added:

Our action will initially be to stop work as usual and to open the campus. An open campus is a place in which all people participate actively in discussion and debate. An open campus does not require the attendance of police or national guardsmen. An open campus needs no formal classes and examinations. At the convocation Wednesday, we hope that the campus community will affirm their determination to enlarge the discussion and debate on Nixon's actions to include the entire Berkeley community (*Daily Californian*, May 5, 1970).

On a cold, overcast Wednesday, 17,000 huddled together at a campuswide convocation in the outdoor Greek Theater. Signs and banners were scattered throughout the audience, some proclaiming that colleges and departments of the university were on strike. A sign on the speaker's podium reminded people to "Forget the Alamo." There were many speakers during the convocation, and a diverse cross section of campus opinion was represented, although all speakers were opposed to the President's decision. Peter Scott and sociology professor Franz Schurmann presented historical analyses of American involvement in Southeast Asia. Mike Tigar, former Berkeley law student and campus activist, spoke about the war from the persepctive of international law: "Today, as in 1966, my president is a war criminal, and my country is an international outlaw" (*Daily Californian*, May 7, 1970). George Pimentel, professor of chemistry, stressed the need for "rationality and not emotionalism" and asked the audience to try to educate congressmen and the public about ". . . the crisis our country faces."

Only two speakers suggested violence as a possible response to the crisis. The first was booed off the stage. The second, Jim Nabors, leader of the previous year's Third World Liberation Front strike, received only scattered applause when he made a reference to violence. He received more support for his demands for the ". . . release of all political prisoners, freedom for Los Siete, withdrawal of American troops from all third world communities, and free passage back to the United States for Eldridge Cleaver" (*Daily Californian*, May 7, 1970).

Highlight of the convocation was the presentation of a proposed declaration of the ad hoc Faculty-Student Peace Committee, called "The Wolin Proposal" after Sheldon Wolin, the professor of political science who was its principal author. The declaration read:

1 This campus is on strike to reconstitute the University as a center for organizing against the war in Southeast Asia. We are curtailing normal activities for the remainder of the quarter. We pledge our time, energy and commitment to stopping this war. We will open the campus to mobilize our resources—our knowledge and skills, our manpower and facilities. We will organize not only against the war, but against the structures in society that facilitate that war. And we will organize to end our University's complicity with that war.

2 We will immediately press to end our University's relationship with ROTC, the Livermore and Los Alamos Laboratories [where war-related research is conducted] and the Thailand Counter Insurgency project.

3 We will organize and cooperate with anti-war activity in the community and across the nation and use the summer to prepare for a national strike, in which colleges and high schools in particular would refuse to resume their normal activities in the fall if the war has not stopped by that time.

4 We will resist with all our resources the repression of anti-war and other dissenting activity, on the campus and off.

5 We will protect ourselves by taking steps to minimize our risks and to aid each other when we engage in necessary risks. We will make every effort to protect the jobs and wages of the University staff and to enable the faculty to discharge the minimum responsibilities required to protect the present and future academic status of students.

6 While our anti-war actions will be disruptive of normal activities, it is not our intention to encourage destructive actions.

7 Following this convocation we will organize ourselves to begin all of these important tasks and will develop proposals for reconstituting the University to these ends. We will meet again Monday to determine together how we will implement the goals set forth in this declaration.

When the proposal had been read, the audience roared its approval. And from the first sentence came the name the Berkeley protest was to be known by, the "reconstitution" or "reconstitution movement."

Most students, faculty, and staff appeared to be impressed with the convocation—the large number of people, the unanimity, the intellectual presentation of the issues, and the lack of radical rhetoric. However, a few activists criticized it as an irrelevant "liberal shuck," and some—like one faculty member who was interviewed—saw it as highly emotional and controlled by individuals trying ". . . to turn the university to their political purposes." It seemed that most members of the university community felt that the Wolin Proposal suggested constructive responses to the crisis. One student said:

The Wolin Proposal gave a handle on action. It was a nonviolent yet radical thing; it was in contrast to trashing [i.e., the violent disruption of classes]. I think that the majority feel the need to to something but not violence; for once there was a plan for what people could do. Most students wanted to do something to stop the war.

Even before the convocation ended early that Wednesday afternoon, Governor Reagan had ordered the campuses of the university and the state colleges closed, and requested the same of private colleges and universities. People of all political persuasions interpreted this as a victory for student activists. Jess Unruh, then the Democratic contender in the gubernatorial race, said that this ". . . was precisely what the radicals wanted" (*Daily Californian*, May 7, 1970). A number of students, however, saw it as an attempt to thwart antiwar protests.

Despite the order to close the campus, students and faculty in many departments met immediately after the campuswide convocation in "departmental convocations." Many of these meetings resulted in votes to condemn the decision to invade Cambodia and in plans for antiwar activities. For example, a Department of Business Administration resolution, passed by a vote of 338 to 35 at a meeting of many of the students and faculty, read: "As an educational branch of the business community, we appeal to the community to express its condemnation of the government's action in Southeast Asia and take positive steps to dissuade Washington from its current divisive course" (*Daily Californian*, May 7, 1970).

On Wednesday night the Strike Coordinating Committee (composed of hastily selected representatives from many campus groups and departments) held a mass meeting to discuss future actions. Over 2,000 people jammed into Pauley Ballroom in the Student Union to participate in the long, disorganized meeting. Most of the discussion centered around which facilities should be used for antiwar activities. According to Governor Reagan's order, only a few campus buildings would be open for the four-day period beginning at midnight, and many students feared that it would not be feasible to organize protest activities off-campus. However, the audience voted overwhelmingly to comply with the Governor's order and avoid possible violence. In particular, a proposal to stage a sit-in was defeated. At the end of the meeting, many organizations and groups announced meeting times and places (many in churches, fraternity houses, and residential cooperatives) and tentative plans for action.

On Friday, May 8, a peaceful demonstration in Sproul Plaza memorialized the four students killed at Kent State. Over 5,000 people attended the demonstration, which included speeches, a 15-minute silent vigil, and hundreds of green picket signs reminding people to "Keep it Cool." The meeting was illegal under Governor Reagan's order, and Chancellor Heyns refused to authorize it but did not call in the police.

In general, Governor Reagan's closing of the university did not hamper the organization of antiwar activities. There were many on-campus buildings available to students and the campus newspaper was published on Sunday under the ad hoc, unofficial title of *The Independent Californian* without the aid of university funds. In fact, many people put more energy into the antiwar activity as the week wore on. One student said: "My God, everywhere I go on campus, in every building, there are hundreds of people doing things. Organizing, meeting, writing leaflets—it's incredible" (*Daily Californian*, May 8, 1970).

One of the most common activities was canvassing—students handed out leaflets and petitions to people in middle-class, black, and industrial communities and talked with them about the war and related social issues. Some students contacted their future colleagues in the society at large—such as businessmen, lawyers, teachers, architects, engineers, and professors at other colleges. Responses to the students varied from a warm eagerness for discussion to open hostility. Generally, people were willing to talk and discussions resulted in greater understanding and openness, if not in agreement. Students' experiences were sometimes satisfying, sometimes frustrating, but they were usually intense. One undergraduate wrote (in a paper submitted for a course in a professional school) about her experiences while canvassing for four days in a black neighborhood:

... I never encountered a single individual there who supported either the Cambodian invasion or the Vietnam war.

When you canvass door-to-door, you are entering someone else's home ground. People are automatically defensive because you are invading their privacy and they usually assume that you're selling something. The effort, by its nature, is more painstaking, more timeconsuming, and less productive in terms of how many letters you collect. But it is the most effective way of communicating with people who don't usually get involved in political action.

There were a lot of retired people in the area, most of them women. Few could read or write ... It was a delicate situation when I interviewed these people because: (1) I was a white female college student; (2) they were very embarrassed that they couldn't read or write. But it was surprising how well informed they were. They all watched the news on television. They could tell me how many troops Nixon promised to withdraw and when he announced the Cambodian invasion, etc. Many were directly affected by the war. They had nephews or grandchildren who had been killed in the war. They were intelligent, warm, good people. I thoroughly enjoyed talking with them.

Many groups on campus wrote letters of protest and attempted to disseminate information about the war. For example, the Berkeley chapter of Concerned Asian Scholars, a national organization, publicly declared: "The present situation demands that as concerned scholars of Asia we devote our energies fully to the accumulation and distribution of information on Cambodia, Laos, Thailand, and Vietnam. Our normal academic efforts cannot be resumed until this task is accomplished" (*Daily Californian*, May 7, 1970). And 22 of the 28 resident faculty and staff of the Center for South and Southeast Asia Studies wrote in a letter to President Nixon:

... This escalation can only bring further destruction of the nations of Southeast Asia and indiscriminate killing of its innocent populations. It also contributes to the perversion of American social and political purposes. As persons representing all shades of political opinion whose professional lives are devoted to teaching and studying the civilizations of South and Southeast Asia, we are convinced that our government's recent policies are disastrous and that this war must stop now (*Daily Californian*, May 8, 1970).

Even some of the more traditional spirit and rally groups on the Berkeley campus issued statements of protest, among them the Oski Dolls:

We, the Oski Dolls and Californians of the University of California at Berkeley, declare our shock and abhorrence at the recent escalation of the war in Southeast Asia. We stand united in opposition to this war and support non-violent constructive action which would speed our withdrawal from that area (*Daily Californian*, May 11, 1970).

In general, protest tactics were moderate. When leafletting industries, engineering students tried ". . . to dress up slightly to more readily identify themselves with the engineering community." The admonition made by an ad hoc group in a social science department was typical: "If your hair or beard is too way-out, and you know whether it is or not, either sacrifice it for a month or two or do not go [canvassing]. Do something else [for the reconstitution movement] instead." Students emphasized that they were making every effort to work through existing channels:

We watch students being shot because "there was no more tear gas"; the President and military decide to control where and when war will be fought; constitutional and international law are defied, and trampled. And we who raise voices of dissent are referred to as "bums" who won't listen to reason. We do not support violence or coercion either from the right or left, so we have resorted to the political channels, which we are so often accused of ignoring, in order to effect our ideas.

Some groups tried to effect change by creating direct political and economic pressure. Some law students went to the state capitol in Sacramento to lobby for antiwar legislation. Another group attempted to organize an economic boycott of products of corporations highly complicit in the war effort. Other groups took a cultural approach and emphasized value conflicts. Students in the Department of Dramatic Art took ". . . plays to the streets, schools, and local theatres in an attempt to inform the community and arouse constructive participation in the antiwar campaign" (*Daily Californian*, May 8, 1970).

Most reconstitution activities were created and coordinated on a decentralized level—by individuals in academic departments and other campus groups, as this excerpt from *The Daily Californian* (May 15, 1970) indicates:

While strike central in Eshleman Hall has received a great deal of attention as the hub of activities, most campus groups have their own strike headquarters.

The strike center in Wheeler Hall is a prime example of such decentralization. Composed mostly of English department students, this organization has taken over most of the rooms on the third floor of the building.

The Wheeler organization is broken up into six groups with one office serving as a strike central.

One of the groups, housed in 306, is in charge of fund-raising for the organization. Through poetry readings, movies and book sales, the Wheeler group has managed to be monetarily self-sufficient.

Other groups on the third floor are working on such activities as community leafletting, working-class organizing, publicizing strike activities, and forming classes in political theory.

Closed for four days, the university officially reopened on Monday, May 11, and the Strike Coordinating Committee held a campuswide mass meeting in Harmon Gymnasium to make decisions about the future of the reconstitution. The meeting began with a long list of speakers, among them Tom Hayden, representatives from the Black Student Union (BSU) and the Women's Liberation, Professor Wolin of the ad hoc Peace Committee, and Dan Siegel, student body president. There was little more than scattered applause for any speaker except Professor Wolin, who ". . . emphasized that a course of moderation and tolerance should be followed in the strike" (*Daily Californian*, May 12, 1970). In fact, students began to leave after the first couple of speeches, and departures continued throughout the meeting, although a majority remained to vote on the proposal presented by the Committee. The proposal read in part:

This campus is on strike to reconstitute the university as a center for organizing against the war in Southeast Asia and against repression at home. We are curtailing normal activities for the remainder of the war. We will open the campus to mobilize our resources—our knowledge and skills, our manpower and facilities. We will organize not only against the war and racism but against the structures in society that facilitate them. We will organize to end our University's complicity with that war and with racial and economic oppression.

A major function of the American university has been to train students to manipulate objects, persons and ideas in ways which support, justify, and implement the American world system. That system results in the exploitation of working people and Third World peoples in this country and the exploitation and forceful suppression of peoples abroad who have been disastrously caught in the brutality of American Imperialism. . . .

A reconstituted university is dedicated to the reversal of the university's normal function. It is dedicated to the enrichment of human life and the enhancement of the scope of human freedom. . . .

(Then the proposal called for the "immediate release of all political prisoners"; an end to the "undeclared war against the Black Panther Party and all other Third World political groups"; establishment of child care centers on campus for students and staff; creation of a women's studies department; and equal voice in decision making for nonacademic staff, students, and faculty—From the *Daily Californian*, May 11, 1970).

The Coordinating Committee recommended that no regular classes be held for the rest of the quarter, that all students receive at least pass grades for the courses in which they were enrolled, and that no member of the faculty or staff "suffer a financial loss from the strike." They also proposed that the implementation of strike policy and the assessment of the strike be left up to each department (*Daily Californian*, May 11, 1970). These proposals were approved. Two minority reports were defeated; one called for the cancellation of all classes, and the other recommended that all decisions about reconstitution be made by the members of each class.

Many of the students, faculty, and staff who agreed with the substance of the Strike Coordinating Committee proposals were bothered by their tone and the tone of the meeting itself. They felt that the meeting, and the wording of the proposals had been dominated by radical rhetoric and conducted in a manipulative way. Some felt that the speakers had been condescending in their arguments on behalf of the proposals. Some students commented that the spirit of the Wolin proposal had been violated, and that the Strike Coordinating Committee had an overrepresentation of militant activists (the nature and operation of the Strike Coordinating Committee will be considered in detail in Chapter 2). Also, some questioned the incorporation of demands by Women's Lib and the BSU into the proposal.

It became increasingly clear that reconstitution activities would be determined in large part by individuals acting within a departmental context. Most departments held meetings to decide what actions to take. An important element in the activity that developed was the official policy of "flexibility," which Chancellor Heyns outlined in a statement to the university community on Monday:

I share the intense concern of all members of the University community about the war, and I understand the widespread and deeply felt desire to modify our usual style of life in the interest of terminating the war. At the same time, the University's educational responsibilities must be safeguarded. These two impulses to modify and to preserve—are not incompatible.

We face an immediate crisis. There are those who advocate closing down the University for the remainder of the academic year. Others propose that we continue business as usual. But by far the largest group in the University community supports an in-between position. Clearly this is the most feasible alternative and the one most responsive to the variety of feelings expressed by the campus community.

There are many different student interests and it will be my position to be as helpful as I can in aiding these diverse interests.

While great flexibility in the organization of courses is permitted and encouraged, I am confident that you [the faculty] will discharge your instructional responsibilities fairly and with proper regard for academic standards. . . .

In this immediate situation, we trust that you [the nonacademic staff] will continue to perform your assigned duties. Should this be personally impossible, we suggest you review with your supervisor the possibility of a leave of absence or participating during non-working hours. . . .

The administration has two primary responsibilities, each of profound importance. First, the University must be preserved as a place where the pursuit of knowledge is the primary concern of both the faculty and students and as a place where reason and intellect above all are honored. Second, the individual rights and privileges of every single member of this complex community must be protected.

. . . But they are not, I believe, inconsistent with many of the extraordinary activities contemplated for the weeks ahead (*Daily Californian*, May 11, 1970).

In line with Chancellor Heyns' statement, the deans of the schools and colleges adopted administrative measures ". . . to provide flexibility for students in adjusting their programs to extraordinary circumstances" (*Daily Californian*, May 11, 1970). Procedures for grading and awarding credit were modified for the duration of the academic quarter.

The most important change was that students were allowed to have all of their courses graded on a "pass/not pass" basis. Normally, undergraduates may take only one "pass/not pass" course per quarter, and it must be a course outside the major field. Graduate students may not usually have their courses graded "pass/not pass." In addition, deadlines for dropping and adding courses were extended almost to the end of the quarter.

The flexible administrative provisions allowed students and faculty to work out programs which satisfied the individual student's needs and interests. Some students chose a full load of independent study courses so they could integrate antiwar activities with their academic pursuits. Some students received partial course credit for work completed in the month of April, and others were allowed to reduce their academic workload by accepting only three units of credit for courses which normally carry five units. In some instances, students received credit for "combined" course work—for their regular work during April and for antiwar related academic work during the reconstitution.

The extent of flexibility varied among faculty members. Some provided special make-up sessions and tutorials for students involved in antiwar activities. Sometimes, students were permitted to extend their course work through the summer and into the fall. This was usually done by giving students a grade of "incomplete," but sometimes sequential courses were restructured so that part of the fall sequence covered material missed in the spring. Some faculty members "reconstituted" their courses to make them more relevant to the antiwar movement and to social change in general. (Adaptations of this latter kind will be considered in subsequent chapters.)

The faculty Senate Committee on Senate Policy also issued a statement, on May 11, on the university's operation through the remainder of the term:

The grave crisis now facing the nation calls upon us, as members of the academic community to organize, to educate and mobilize others, and to exert all legitimate pressure to change the course of the nation's war policies. . . .

The best way that the academic community can demonstrate that there are civilized roads to a more responsible society is to stay open. The continuation of the University as an intellectual center does not in any way diminish the effectiveness of those who would not only explore ideas but apply them to the solution of the crisis we face (*Daily Californian*, May 11, 1970).

Indeed most members of the university felt the institution should be kept open. However, there were disagreements about what the nature of the curriculum should be and about who should make decisions about the curriculum. For example, the ad hoc Faculty-Student Peace Committee took the position that courses should continue but should be made relevant to the current social crisis. Moreover, they felt that students and staff, in addition to the faculty, should help determine the content of courses. They recommended the following guidelines for the reconstitution:

1 Every class should discuss the relation of the course's substance to the present foreign and domestic crisis and should seek ways of making the substance relevant to the crisis, including the way of seeking the deeper roots of the crisis itself. . . .

2 Every class should resolve these matters by decisions arrived at by intensive and open discussion among faculty, students, and staff. No one person or group should impose a framework by fiat.

3 We encourage peaceful picketing and leafletting in the vicinity of class-rooms by students, faculty, and staff as an appropriate response to classes which continue their business-as-usual. . . . The purpose of picketing is not to coerce but to demonstrate a moral commitment to ending the War and to persuade others of the rightness of that commit-ment (*Daily Californian*, May 15, 1970).

The ad hoc faculty Council for an Academic Community, on the other hand, expressed the view that the faculty had the responsiblity to continue with the normal curriculum, even though flexibility and some course modifications were appropriate. The Council added that only the faculty should have the authority to determine curriculum. Their statement on "Academic Freedom and Integrity" was signed by several hundred of the almost 2,000 faculty members on the Berkeley campus. It read in part:

. . . as we adjust schedules and examinations this quarter to accommo-date widespread political concerns in our community, we must also reaffirm those principles which are the necessary mark of a free univer-sity.

The right of students, even if they are a minority in a class, to continue to meet with their teacher is not subject to a vote. . . .

Second, no teacher should abandon his responsibility in teaching his course by altering its content in order to satisfy the political interests of a segment of his students—whether they are a minority or a majority of his class—(although this statement does not reflect on the propriety of course modifications in the present circumstances in ways germane to the subject matter and proper course content consistent with the teacher's pedagogical responsibility). . . .

Moreover, we believe that our effectiveness in exercising our rights as citizens in the present crisis will be enhanced by our refraining from exploiting our classrooms as political forums.

It is only on these conditions that we can defend our rights as a free academic community from outside political interference (*Daily Californian*, May 21, 1970).

In some cases, classes that continued as usual were picketed. Teaching assistants in the campus chapter of the American Federation of Teachers had voted on May 8 to picket classrooms and buildings in support of the Wolin proposal. On Sunday, May 10, over 60 people in the People's Coalition voted to allow classes to meet on Monday without disruption, but by Thursday, May 14, People's Coalition and some ad hoc departmental strike committees had disrupted a few classes. The usual tactic was to shout down a professor until he would share equal privileges with students in discussing the reconstitution and in deciding whether or not to disband or modify the class (*Daily Californian*, May 14, 1970). These protestors felt that their tactics were less coercive than the unilateral decisions by some faculty to continue with business as usual. One student wrote, ". . . attempts to conduct 'business as usual' on the basis of academic freedom must be opposed—such actions are sophisticated efforts to perpetuate the absolute power of one side" (*Daily Californian*, May 11, 1970).

Some faculty, students, and staff saw the classroom disruptions as part of a coercive attempt by antiwar protestors to politicize the university. For example, an ad hoc group of about a dozen students (mostly from one humanities department), called Students for an Academic Community, issued this statement:

While concerned Americans are presently stunned by the political and social holocaust overwhelming this nation, we, students and staff of the University of California at Berkeley, refuse to add to the escalation of chaos.

Recent trends here and elsewhere toward disruption, anarchy, violence and arbitrary "redirection" of classes, are concrete threats to the American concept of a non-partisan University and more immediately to the existence of this institution. . . .

However, most students, faculty, and staff agreed that, in purpose and practice, the reconstitution was nonviolent and generally noncoercive. One faculty member said the students were ". . . assertive but not strident." Another suggested:

It may be said that individuals are becoming post-bureaucratic men and women, that they are taking responsibilities for their own decisions—that they are making moral choices, instead of employing rigid formulas. Individuals are more respecting of the dignity of others; 'coercion' is only by example and moral persuasion.

During the first two weeks of reconstitution, roughly one-third of the student body spent most of their time participating in reconstitution activities, another third spent some time in these activities, and the remaining third was generally apathetic or uninvolved. (A substantial number of faculty and nonacademic staff—perhaps a majority—were sympathetic to at least some of the reconstitution activities, but few spent large portions of their time participating.) Subsequently, the numbers of students participating began to decrease sharply. Some students took time off from classes to go to the beach or to read. Students participating in antiwar activities began to get frustrated.

Near the end of May 1970, only about one-third of the student body was active in any kind of reconstitution activity, and only a very small percentage were devoting most of their time to reconstitution efforts. Five thousand people attended the second campuswide convocation on May 27, but the atmosphere was one of lethargy. The audience was not interested in the speakers, and was neither responsive nor enthusiastic. Some people still hoped that the reconstitution could be continued through the summer and into the fall. On May 29 about 100 representatives from various campus groups and departments attended a meeting and discussed plans for summer and fall activities.

On June 4, students held a noon reaffirmation rally in Sproul Plaza. During the rally the crowd listening to the speakers increased from a couple of hundred to perhaps 2,000. The speakers talked about what had been learned during the past month and about plans for the future. Professor Wolin said that the reconstitution had put some pressure on Nixon to end the war and had begun to change the university by helping people break out of established routines. He said that the reconstitution helped reduce barriers between students, faculty, and staff, and between the university and the community. Professor Wolin said that educational reform must continue, but that efforts to end the war must also continue. He then proposed that on October 2 everyone come together to decide what to do about continuing the reconstitution, and that a constitutional convention of the campus be convened at the end of the winter quarter, 1971.

Rick Brown, a student who had played an active leadership role on the ad hoc Peace Committee and on the Strike Coordinating Committee, noted that thousands of students, faculty, and staff had become politically involved for the first time during the reconstitution. Brown said that:

Many worked in electoral politics, not realizing that one man can't effect change. . . . The lesson we've learned is the need for collective action and responsibility. . . . What we've learned this past month are the conditions of violence and peace that can bring us together.

He also proposed that colleges and universities should be made "centers of struggle"—for self-determination of Third World peoples (at home, in Southeast Asia, and elsewhere), for freedom for political prisoners, for an end to university complicity with the war, and for an end to discrimination (e.g., against women and the poor). He suggested that the university be organized according to these different centers of struggle, instead of according to academic departments.

After the reaffirmation rally, people visited an "activities fair" where information was available on activities planned for the summer. Activities included: speaking to unions and labor groups, professional organizations, law enforcement agencies, industries, and workers at Livermore Laboratory (where war-related research is conducted); canvassing door-to-door; working on draft and tax resistance; attempting a consumer boycott of defense contractors; performing antiwar benefit plays and poetry readings; researching university complicity in the war; working at a black community center in West Berkeley (including drug education and recreational programs for youth); lobbying in Sacramento; and planning new academic programs in some departments for the fall.

While many of the summer activities were implemented, they generally took place on a small scale. And when students returned in the fall, there was a widespread feeling that the reconstitution hadn't really made any difference. The war was continuing, and the United States had escalated the bombing over Cambodia when the troops were withdrawn. The vote on the McGovern-Hatfield amendment had been postponed for several months, weakened by amendments, and finally defeated. At the beginning of September, one university staff member commented: "Summer tends to make this world unreal. Upon return this fall, many may walk through the campus and wonder if maybe last spring was a dream. They may find it difficult to believe that once, only four months ago, the campus was so filled with hope and activity."

In general, there was a return to normalcy in the fall. The "Day of Decision" scheduled for October 2 was never held. And the Regents, the university administration, and the faculty adopted regulations designed to reduce the likelihood of another "reconstitution." At the direction of the Regents and President Charles Hitch, head of the University of California system, Chancellor Heyns issued a list of

"Guidelines on Use of University Facilities" in order to ". . . ensure that personal political activity (1) will not be mistaken for University activity, (2) will not involve the use of University funds, facilities, equipment, materials or other institutional resources, and (3) will not intrude upon the instructional program and other operations of the University." Also, disciplinary actions were taken against a few faculty members for "reconstituting" their courses. And the Faculty Senate Committee on Courses issued a.directive emphasizing that independent study credit should not be given to students wishing to participate in ad hoc courses (as had sometimes been the case in the past, and particularly during the reconstitution).

A number of students and faculty voiced concern that these new guidelines were being used to ban political signs from dormitory windows, to question the appropriateness of voter registration campaigns on campus, and to intimidate faculty and students trying to initiate more socially relevant courses. Toward the end of October, a mass meeting was held to protest governmental and university repression of activists. Only 1,200 students attended, and most were bored with the speeches—everyone was interested only in "his own thing," whether it was talking into the microphone, proselytizing for various political groups, or just "rapping" with friends.

Meanwhile, at the request of the Regents and the university administration, the faculty were developing a code of conduct to govern their professional behavior. After months of discussion, the faculty adopted a code similar to that recommended by the American Association of University Professors. The code attempts to outline a separation of personal political activity from professional and institutional activity. Some faculty members objected to it on the grounds that: "The guidelines will be used selectively to punish people with unpopular political views" (*Daily Californian*, October 27, 1970). However, most faculty agreed with it—some out of apathy, some out of the fear that the Regents might confront them with a less acceptable code, and many because they felt that the code was necessary to the preservation of an academic institution.

However, the power to determine the official status of ROTC was removed from faculty hands by the Regents and the administration, as reported in the *Daily Californian* (October 19, 1970):

On September 17, the Regents adopted a report submitted by University President Charles Hitch recommending that "ROTC curricula not be substantially different this year than it was last year." Further, the courses for 1971-1972 will be drawn up and submitted through the Chancellor and the President to the Board of Regents in February, 1971. President Hitch and the Regents have both pledged to continue and improve the ROTC programs.

This decision countered a vote by the Berkeley Academic Senate on May 18 to phase out credit for ROTC.

For the most part, decisions made on the campuswide level since reconstitution have tended to support the status quo, as the above examples indicate. However, in some cases reconstitution may have stimulated further decentralized antiwar activities and educational reform (see Chapter 3). The trend seems to be toward change through relatively small groups—political communes, study-action groups, and "radical" caucuses within academic departments.

Scientists and Engineers for Social and Political Action (SESPA) has continued to work for the discontinuation of war-related research on the campus (particularly at Livermore Laboratory) and for permission to hold political discussions at campus science laboratories. Thus far, the Chancellor and the faculty Academic Freedom Committee have recommended that sociopolitical discussions and meetings be allowed at the Lawrence Radiation Laboratory during the noon hour. A group of students are organizing an institute that will offer credit for practical political research. Its aim will be to help students ". . . be effective in the world of practical politics" (e.g., polltaking, effective canvassing). It does not aim to support any particular ideology or candidate, and has the support of students and faculty representing a variety of political perspectives (*Daily Californian*, October 12, 1970).

The reconstitution may also have increased student participation in campaigns for local political offices. Students participated heavily in three recent elections. In the California Sixteenth Assembly District, Ken Meade, a liberal Democrat, gave the Democrats control of the State Assembly with an upset victory over the incumbent, a conservative Republican. And in the local congressional race, Ron Dellums, a very liberal Democrat (some might say "radical") became the first black man elected to Congress from a predominantly white district. In the April 6 city elections, a coalition of activist blacks and whites elected three of their four candidates to the City Council. Rick Brown, a student leader during the reconstitution, missed election by a very narrow margin.

The reconstitution seems to have been the beginning of a trend toward greater student involvement in local politics, in small political and educational groups, and in academic reform on the departmental level. In order to better understand the reconstitution, it will be necessary to consider in more depth and detail the activities and processes within some of the departments and groups which served as centers for participation in this attempt at social and educational change.

2. Departments and Groups: Centers of Action and Interaction

Like many others, I was impressed with activities of the reconstitution. I saw students, faculty, and staff of many political persuasions come together to work for the improvement of the university and the society. In a number of situations, conditions for learning seemed much better than usual. Many students and faculty appeared to be learning more about the educational process, the conditions of the larger society, and about the subject matter and methods of their academic disciplines. There were many open and intense discussions of educational and social problems, and attempts to formulate and experiment with possible solutions. One student said: "There has been more education in the past month [May] than all the learning in a [regular] course could make up for. I feel like my education's just begun."

Moreover, people seemed to have hope that change was possible and that it could be achieved in a constructive, nonviolent way. These impressions gave me hope, and by May 7, I was working with a couple of campus groups. At the Center for Research and Development in Higher Education, I served on the ad hoc antiwar steering committee.

While participating in these activities, I began to wonder how this situation had been created and how we might evaluate our efforts. So I decided to initiate a study of the reconstitution. It was my hope that people at Berkeley and other universities and colleges, as well as members of the society at large, might learn something about higher education and society from such a study. I recruited 30 people to help me conduct interviews and participant-observations in a number of campus departments and groups. Most of these people were involved in some reconstitution activities and were committed to learning more about what was happening. Indeed, their beliefs about the reconstitution often changed as a result of the research.

Most of the members of the research team were educational researchers or graduate students in education, and most had previous interviewing experience. However, in some respects the group was quite diverse. All were opposed to the war, but they had many shades of political opinion. A few were graduating seniors about 21, and several were graduate students over 40 with families. In fact, there was one mother-daughter team on the research staff. A couple were members of the nonacademic staff and two were student personnel administrators.

We interviewed students, faculty, and staff in 34 academic departments, and several other campus groups. The interviewees were used as informants about the activities, processes, and issues they thought most important to the situation in their department or group, and in the university as a whole, during the reconstitution. Each interviewer was given a 10-page mimeographed interview form. However, they were encouraged to be flexible in conducting interviews—the information obtained in early interviews and observations often suggested new questions and lines of inquiry. Thus, the members of the research group added, altered, and eliminated questions in light of emerging and changing hypotheses developed during the progress of the data collection.[1] I also consulted with each interviewer during and after the data collection, which extended from the middle of May to the middle of June. We discussed the meaning of consistencies and inconsistencies in their findings, and occasionally conducted an extra interview to fill in a gap in our information.

We attempted to study a diverse sample of departments and groups, including some of the less active groups. In obtaining a cross section of departments, we considered their subject-matter (i.e., humanities, social sciences, natural sciences, and professions) and general level of involvement in the reconstitution (based on information from the Strike Coordinating Committee). We conducted from four to seven interviews with some participant observation in 14 academic departments, and from one to five interviews without participant observation in 20 academic departments.[2]

During our first interviews, we found that public information about the "strike status" of departments was often inaccurate and tended to make ad hoc agreements appear official. For example, concerning some departments which continued with only minor changes in their normal operations, such statements as the following were sometimes publicized (*Daily Californian*, May 11, 1970):

[1] For a theoretical and methodological explanation and justification for this procedure, see Blumer, 1969, pp. 1-60.

[2] Immediately after collecting interview and participant-observation data, we assigned each department a number within a broad subject matter area to ensure anonymity. For example, the political science department might have been labeled "social science department # 2," or the engineering department labeled "science oriented professional department # 3." (Other categories included humanities, natural sciences, and socially oriented professions.)

Decision to strike; final decisions concerning curtailment of activities left up to classes.

The Department had a small meeting after the convocation; voted to strike indefinitely.

Usually, however, a department's position could be clearly stated only by including more detail in the announcements, as in this example:

Departmental members (faculty, staff, employees, students) voted on Tuesday to endorse the Ad Hoc Student-Faculty Committee's resolutions. The meeting was *not* officially endorsed by the departmental chairman, and as yet he does *not* consider the department on strike. The support for a strike is held by a majority of department members.

In studying each of the departments and groups in our sample, we made an effort to talk with individuals representing a wide variety of perspectives. Roughly 60 percent of the interviewees were students, about 30 percent were faculty, and 10 percent were nonacademic staff. About half of those interviewed were deeply involved in the reconstitution effort, one-quarter were opposed, and another one-quarter were minimally involved or relatively apathetic. We studied 34 academic departments, some residence halls, the campuswide Strike Coordinating Committee, the Peace Brigade, Third World Students, and varsity athletes; in addition, we obtained information about the campus movement as a whole.

The responses of the academic departments to the events of May 1970 were quite diverse. However, three themes—"stability," "flexibility and activist separatism," and "experimentation"—characterized the different patterns of activity and processes of change observed in most departments. More than 12 of the 34 departments are best characterized by "stability"; most of these are in the humanities, sciences, and science-oriented professions. The majority are best characterized by "flexibility and activist separatism"; they represent a cross section of disciplines and professions. And while only one of the departments is best characterized by "experimentation," about 10 of those in the second category showed important aspects of this theme; most of these departments are in the social sciences and socially oriented professions.

An examination of three hypothetical departments, each of which is actually a composite of academic departments we studied, provides a better understanding of the range of departmental activity and processes of change encountered during the reconstitution. The three hypothetical departments are not "typical," of course, because in the nature of this kind of analysis, the combination of activities and characteristics of several actual departments intensifies and extends the characteristics and activities of the model. In the descriptions that follow, Department A illustrates the theme of "stability," Department B illustrates "flexibility and activist separatism," and Department C illustrates "experimentation."

DEPARTMENT A:
STABILITY

Before the reconstitution, few of the students in Department A had been involved in political activism, and only a few faculty and students had shown any interest in educational reform. Most students and faculty saw the reconstitution as a short-range activity. Many of the students felt that May 1970 was a time of national crisis and that all citizens should express their concern with the direction in which the country was moving.

A mass meeting open to all students, faculty, and staff in the department took place immediately after the campuswide convocation on May 6. A small group of graduate students had called for the meeting the previous day. This was the first time students had organized any departmentwide meeting, and the first time that members of the nonacademic staff had been invited to attend a meeting with faculty and students. One-third of the students and staff and one-half of the faculty in the department attended the meeting. A wide cross section of departmental membership was represented, although there was an especially high proportion of students, faculty, and staff interested in participating in antiwar acitivty. Also, a higher percentage of graduate students attended than undergraduates.

Almost everyone agreed that official departmental decisions could not be made at the meeting, since only the faculty had the power to set departmental policies. Moreover, the chairman said he would close any meeting at which an effort was made to take a strike vote. He maintained that no vote or discussion could alter the faculty's institutionally defined responsibilities and that even an unofficial vote would be intimidating to those who wished to continue with their normal activities. As a result, there was no discussion of the Wolin proposal. Those attending the meeting did, as an ad hoc group, pass a resolution condemning President Nixon's decision to invade Cambodia; the vote was nearly unanimous.

At the end of the meeting, several ad hoc committees were formed. Most of their antiwar activities involved canvassing and leafletting in surrounding communities and writing letters to elected officials. Also, some faculty and students contacted fellow professionals outside the university and urged them to help stop the war. Decisions about "reconstituting" classes ". . . were left up to the individual professor, and most students were pretty satisfied with this." In one case, a faculty member did present his class with several alternatives for reconstitution, but the class voted to continue as usual.

Most faculty emphasized the importance of allowing students to continue with business as usual if they wished, even though they often devoted a couple of class sessions to discussing the Cambodian invasion and the national situation. One or two faculty members did permit students to write papers which integrated the concerns of their academic discipline with their antiwar activities. And some faculty held make-up sessions for students who had missed class because of their reconstitution activities. However, after a week or two, most faculty were proceeding with exams and assignments as usual. Although several members of the nonacademic staff wanted to participate in antiwar activities, the chairman required that they perform their normal duties. During their breaks, some secretaries helped students type letters and stuff envelopes (students bought the supplies with their own money).

For two weeks, about 10 percent of the students in the department participated in reconstitution activities. They discussed with each other the issues surrounding the national situation, and some discussed areas of needed educational reform with a few faculty. But the students soon found themselves very tired and under the pressure of having to complete course requirements they had been neglecting. By the end of May, the activity in Department A had returned to normal. A few students had become more socially aware and more interested in future sociopolitical involvement. And perhaps the dialogue on national and educational issues became more intense and informed than before. But the situation in the department remained relatively stable throughout the reconstitution. Only a few people had been intensely involved in antiwar activities, and most made only minor departures from their regular routines.

DEPARTMENT B:
FLEXIBILITY
AND
ACTIVIST
SEPARATISM

The educational attitudes of the students and faculty in this department are quite diverse—ranging from traditional to very change-oriented. Their political attitudes are less diverse but still vary considerably. The majority believe that change can usually be achieved by working within the system. Most students and faculty were outraged by the Cambodian invasion and the Kent State slayings, and many favored some form of reconstitution.

Some graduate students asked the chairman to convene the department for a meeting on the afternoon of May 6, before the campuswide convocation. Almost half of the graduate students, over one-quarter of the undergraduates, half of the faculty, and many nonacademic staff attended the meeting. Most of the students supported the Wolin proposal, but the faculty were more reluctant to endorse it. After considerable debate, about half of the faculty agreed to go along with an endorsement of the Wolin proposal, if the word "strike" were deleted and if an amendment were added to reaffirm academic freedom and the right of individuals to continue with their regular academic work. These compromise amendments were acceptable to most students, except for some activists who believed that the word "strike" contributed to campus solidarity. Also, a few students had hoped for official departmental support of the Wolin proposal.

The main result was the adoption of a strategy of flexibility—an agreement to "live and let live." One student's view was that:

The individual student should decide for himself whether or not to go to class. And the instructor should decide whether or not to teach his class, and whether or not to give credit for reconstitution kinds of activities. I believe in the freedom of individuals to decide these matters for themselves.

The faculty in the department formalized this principle by issuing the following statement:

It is assumed that whatever solution is adopted in each case [i.e., in each class], it will be sufficiently flexible to allow responsible, individual participants to pursue agreed alternative solutions. The faculty respects the right of students who wish to complete the regular work in their courses, and will make appropriate arrangements to enable them to do so. We respect equally the right of students who wish to devote their full time to antiwar activities, and will make accommodations to enable them to do this without loss of credit.

In this department there was little dialogue between individuals of substantially different views. While some faculty and students made plans to conduct their own academic activities as usual, activists began to organize to oppose the war. Neither group discussed the possible implications of their activities with the other.

At the departmental mass meeting, a steering committee was formed. In practice, participation on the steering committee was open to anyone who was interested. However, the views of undergraduates, faculty, staff, and political moderates were underrepresented. One member of the departmental steering committee said:

We on the steering committee feel very removed from most students. For one thing, it was unfortunate that the leadership was taken by grad students at the beginning and the larger amounts of time and energy which could be devoted by undergraduates has been lost. As it is, [we] . . . are operating in a vacuum out of touch with most students.

The members of the steering committee decided that they should take a leadership role and organize individuals who might be interested in reconstitution activities. They issued a statement urging faculty and students to reconstitute their classes. Many faculty reacted strongly to this pressure; they maintained that the steering committee was violating the agreement that each person could do as he pleased. On the other hand, the steering committee felt that the organization of collective action aimed at social and educational change was consistent with the endorsement of the Wolin proposal. The possibility of such incompatibilities had been ignored at the departmental meeting on May 6. It had been assumed that individuals could act in accordance with their own definition of the reconstitution and that they need not discuss the implications of their actions for each other. This assumption led to misunderstandings when the lines of action taken by different individuals and groups conflicted.

These conflicts were resolved with a minimum of dialog. Using their institutional authority, the faculty insisted that activists make their activities clearly separate from departmental functioning. In letters to professional organizations, activists had to make it very clear that they did not represent the department, nor even the majority of individuals in it. Moreover, they were told not to ask professors to reconstitute their classes. One participant-observer noted that:

... [the majority of faculty view reconstitution as] a short-term change in curriculum which allows students to apply their energies in a direction which is most relevant to them in a time of national crisis. Nobody seems to have confidence in any long-range educational reform.

Indeed, there were many difficulties involved in trying to "reconstitute" the curriculum to make it more relevant to social issues. Some faculty and students felt that academic activities should transcend social concerns, that academic activities must not be action-oriented, and that students should be given credit only for academic activities. Some students (including many activists) were so disillusioned with and frustrated by the university curriculum that they thought it was not possible for the university to become socially relevant, even though they felt this was desirable.

Some students and faculty did see the possibility of making the curriculum more relevant to those concerned with creating a better society. For example, one professor provided his large lecture class with several alternatives for reconstituting the course. Most of the students went out into many relatively remote northern California communities to talk with citizens about the war and related issues. Before going into a community, the students did research not only on the war but also on the specific concerns and nature of the community. Once in the community, the students applied their background information and theories of social interaction in dialogs with the local citizens.

But generally, the reconstitution activities in Department B took place outside the context of the official curriculum; this may be called the strategy of "activist separatism." A number of students participated in antiwar activities without receiving academic credit. There were a few socially relevant student-initiated courses; and in a few cases, sympathetic professors gave students academic credit for participating in these ad hoc "courses."

The antiwar activities were coordinated by the ad hoc departmental steering committee, which helped to facilitate intradepartmental communication by posting information and distributing leaflets. It also established grievance procedures to protect students, faculty, and staff who wished to deviate from their normal academic routines.

It was difficult for many students to find ways in which they could become intensely involved in one or two reconstitution activities for more than a couple of days. Those who had initiated reconstitution activities were sometimes cliquish, and often reserved the most interesting and creative tasks for themselves and their friends. Other students were often channeled into the more menial tasks (such as envelope stuffing) without regard to their needs or interests. The following statements by interviewees are typical descriptions of the situation:

When I approached the table where work assignments were made, I was told to return in half an hour because there were no requests in except for canvassers. I stood around for a bit observing the goings-on, until I overheard a request for a typist . . . [People in the dorms would go look for some work, but] they worked for about a half hour and then some of the other people there [who were coordinating activities] told them to come back later when there was something more to do.

A lot of students wanted to get involved but couldn't get involved because they didn't know people well—their services were volunteered but not accepted:

I was working on an etching for the summer national antiwar exhibit. When I got back after my week of sickness, everything was used up and a mess. I was intimidated because I was working alone and not with a group. People snubbed me because I continued to work on my etching—it was an antiwar etching, but they didn't even bother to find out. . . . When I did offer my services at first, I didn't seem to be needed. I went into postering, and there were too many people, and they said to come back later. Then I lost interest, but later people started complaining because there was no one around to help them.

There was little interaction between people working on different projects; and often communication among people working on the same project was poor. The more experienced activists formed a "radical caucus," and a few of the more persistent moderates initiated "within the system" antiwar activities. But the "radicals" and the "moderates" did not cooperate and they reacted somewhat negatively to each other.

After about two weeks, virtually all of the students in Department B had returned to their usual activities. The initial novelty and excitement of the reconstitution had worn off, and finals were approaching. More importantly, most people had been working on reconstitution activities by themselves or in small, closed groups, and they missed the social support that comes from having worked with a number of individuals cooperatively involved in a common enterprise.

As people began to return to their usual academic activities, some students and faculty expressed disappointment that there hadn't been any visible changes in the department. In a departmental meeting in June, one student said:

> Reconstitution means students must be brought into the decision-making process, regarding the uses and orientation of research, the determination of curriculum. Reconstitution is more than receiving pass/not pass grades, than being let out of class to fight the war, than being invited to a departmental colloquium.

Many students felt that the faculty's flexibility had been a token gesture that also protected the existing departmental system—". . . reconstitution was just 'waited out' by those in charge." Some activists and faculty came to be more mistrusting of one another, and to feel that their ideals and interests were irreconcilable.

On the other hand, those students, faculty, and staff who had participated in reconstitution activities developed closer relationships. When students and faculty considered together how they should adapt their class to the crisis situation, they began to respect each other and to understand the diversity of needs and perspectives represented by the other members of the class. Faculty members sometimes showed greater concern for the individual needs of students, and they began to listen to ideas about improving the learning process. These individuals broke out of their normal routines for a couple of weeks, and they experimented with new forms of curricula and new styles of student-faculty relationships. One faculty member said:

> There will be changes in individual approaches to education. My classes will change. We will defy the structure imposed upon us by the classroom. I look upon the teacher as being more a resource than an authority. Students will look at teachers in different ways. The whole experience has been humanizing to a large extent. Roles have been altered and broken. Grades as a system of rewards and punishment will have their eventual abolition hurried by reconstitution.

One student felt that the most important effect of the month was for students to ". . . see professors as people who can be spoken to and even criticized. I'll never feel comfortable in a lecture hall again."

In the department as a whole, there was no improvement in the quality of dialog on issues surrounding educational reform. Disagreements continued to be glossed over in meetings. A departmentwide meeting was held in June to discuss the implications of the reconstitution for educational reform in the department. It was attended by a diverse group of about 100 students, faculty, and staff. The moderator of the discussion consistently broke in and stopped any dialog which got close to revealing fundamental differences of opinion. At one point, a faculty member said: "Faculty and students are closer together than we sound." However, having previously interviewed some of the discussants, it was my feeling that they were further apart than they sounded. At the end of the meeting, one staff member commented: "It's hard for me to speak out because points have been made so bureaucratically [impersonally] and politely."

DEPARTMENT C: EXPERIMENTATION

The social and political orientations of the students and faculty in this department are diverse and similar to those of the faculty and students in Department B. The faculty are more open to educational innovation than the faculty in Department B; in particular, their academic perspectives are more interdisciplinary, and they are more concerned with the social relevance of the university. The department has a history of social involvement and curricular innovation during the past few years. Student-faculty relationships have been generally close and cooperative, although there have been some important tensions and disagreements about issues of departmental curriculum and governance.

After the Kent State slayings, a mass meeting was scheduled in the department for Tuesday, May 5. One-quarter of the students, faculty, and staff in the department attended the meeting and unanimously passed a resolution against the war. The following day, they marched to the campuswide convocation at the Greek Theater in a contingent. Immediately after the convocation, a mass meeting of members of the department endorsed the Wolin proposal. The faculty of the department subsequently endorsed the proposal.

Many students and faculty saw the reconstitution as an opportunity to reevaluate their curriculum and to make it more socially relevant. In marked contrast to Department B, the students and faculty of Department C engaged in dialog on substantive issues of educational change from the beginning of the reconstitution. Faculty and students in the department as a whole and in individual classes jointly determined how the curriculum could be made more relevant for the remainder of the quarter and for the future. They used the intellectual skills and perspectives of their academic field to work for ending the war and improving the society in general. For example, students in a professional school made a course on school design more relevant by ". . . designing and building child care centers in Berkeley and Oakland. Reconstitution for them has meant transformation from an academic approach to involvement in real projects" (From an ad hoc group's printed matter).

About half of the students and faculty were involved in reconstitution activities. Although the level of activity decreased after three weeks, many remained involved until the end of the quarter in mid-June, partly because some of the activities had been integrated into the curriculum. One of the distinctive features of Department C was the massive collective action which created a sense of community among the members of the department. One student said: "At first, I hadn't planned on striking for the whole quarter. . . . I wouldn't have gotten as active if I hadn't been involved in my department where everyone was active." Another said that ". . . the collective energy released through antiwar activity over the past week would embarrass a quarter's classroom productivity."

Action-groups were formed by individuals interested in participating in a given activity. There was the feeling that ". . . if a person can't find a place to plug in, he can create his own niche" (From printed matter of an ad hoc group in the department). Those individuals most involved in a particular situation or activity made the decisions directly affecting that situation. Activities were developed according to the ". . . will and commitment of the people, with leadership emerging as situations dictate" (*Ibid.*).

Activists in Department C sought the participation and involvement of individuals from outside as well as inside. Forms passed out to students solicited their views and suggestions about the reconstitution of the department, and invited them to sign up for activities in which they were interested. One student was impressed when: "People listened to me even though I wasn't a member of the department."

Information was channeled through a steering committee which held coordinating sessions to prevent duplication and keep everyone informed of what others were doing. Informational leaflets were published every couple of days; they played a key role in solidifying people, informing them, and building a greater sense of pride in the numerous activities. One student described the situation this way: "Working groups are held together in a loosely-organized communication and support network which attempts to organize activities so that functions do not overlap needlessly."

Also, some students started a departmental newspaper with the goals of ". . . mobilizing [people] to action on a continuing basis" and to help realize the possibility of a true college community, not in complete harmony but a ". . . pluralistic society with mutual tolerance for differing opinions" (*Ibid.*). People in Department C were very concerned with group processes; the main concern was with the quality of collective and individual participation, rather than with the end product alone. Consider one observer's description of a group problem-solving meeting:

> The group sat quietly around the table, letting the answers slowly evolve—not pushing the striving to make decisions. The purpose of this division is to encourage those persons in it to act according to where they are and so the group acts and thinks quietly to move and decide cautiously, while striving to feel exactly what they're feeling.

In general, the members of Department C were committed to experimentation, to discussing and trying out alternative action projects and educational innovations. There was no consensus on a specific program of reform and action, but there was a general commitment to participation in an ongoing process of change. This is illustrated by a description of project functioning during the reconstitution:

> Free criticism is encouraged to keep ideas from becoming bogged down in procedure. A major goal is to enjoy one's tasks and to learn from them. To prevent stagnation, various groups have begun to rotate positions to allow new ideas and faces to flow from one group to another and to prevent bureaucratic entrenchment of ideas and people in single positions . . . the rotation plan is a fantastic way to keep the [reconstitution] movement from stagnating (*Ibid.*).

A proposed method for curriculum development provides another example of this experimental approach (From student interviewee):

> One person sets up a program and others help to develop the idea. A group evaluates through role playing the process and the program. This essentially institutionalizes a sounding board for curriculum development.

Toward the end of the quarter, the faculty approved an experimental curricular program, emphasizing mutual student-faculty responsibility. The goal of the program was stated as follows:

> [To] Create a reality of co-operative experience in place of "competitive education" by abolishing the concepts of reward and punishment, degrees, and titles. These are distinctive, synthetic barriers between fellow humans who are all engaged in a life-long learning process (Printed matter of ad hoc group in Department C).

> The . . . [program] will not be bound by quarters, units, or grades. But you can petition for a grade for your work, if you want it . . . People will probably work in groups on projects, for the most part. Students will contract with individual faculty members for assistance on specific projects for specific lengths of time. There is some discussion now on whether evaluation should be done by the group working on a specific

project or by a specific faculty member for the students he has contracted to work with (From student interviewee).

It should be noted that people in the department did not always engage in open discussions; some dissension was suppressed. Some students were requested not to attend a faculty meeting in order to avoid polarizing students and faculty. One student said that he was among a minority of students who wanted ". . . to attempt immediate implementation of the most radical proposal, realizing it may cause considerable hostility and opposition from the existing power structure." He added that most students wanted ". . . to make changes only at the rate that they believed would be tolerated by the existing structure."

However, many students claimed that they were not merely trying for "change-by-compromise," but that their main concern was to engage all the members in the department in dialog on substantive social and educational issues. Indeed, one interviewer noted that, ". . . even conservative faculty are closer to students because they had to come together and decide what to do; they had to work things out." Another person believed that sometimes ". . . reconstitution brought to a head what was crying out, changed what should have been changed, now, in a friendly way."

Yet, toward the end of the quarter, some students who had been very optimistic about the possibilities for change began to feel despair, frustration, and disillusionment because substantive departmental change had not yet taken place. Two students wrote the following commentaries:

Student-faculty relations . . . which had reached a high point of common purpose in the aftermath of the Cambodian invasion, slipped well below their normal state of uncertain truce last Thursday, June 11 (Printed matter of an ad hoc group in Department C).

I believe there are double agents and saboteurs who are destroying our efforts to reconstitute. It is typical of each college to thwart creative drive.

Each of us who has not participated but who wants a better life, a better society is a saboteur; each of us who has participated but has made decisions for other students and says he wants 'student control' is a double agent. We are being dissipated—co-opted. This is supposed to be student designed/cooperative education (*Ibid.*).

It is clear that the situation in Department C was very complex. The scale of antiwar activity and the extent of educational reform was much greater than in Departments A and B. Also, more than other departments, there was a sense of community, at least for awhile. It is also clear that experimentation was not as extensive as many had expected.

Yet, a number of faculty and students remain open (if not committed) to experimenting with new educational and social alternatives. One student said about the faculty in Department C: "They're beginning to accept that they don't know something for sure."

STRIKE
COORDINATING
COMMITTEES

The reconstitution was basically a decentralized movement. As stated before, most activities originated in academic departments or through various student groups. There were some outstanding instances of interdepartmental and intergroup collaboration, much more than is usual for the university. For example, 15 students from the departments of landscape architecture, zoology, and biology participated in an interdisciplinary course on the effects of the war on the Vietnamese landscape. They collected:

. . . information on the Indochinese landscape, including crater-marked landscape, herbicidal defoliation, as well as the quality and quantity of California land owned by the military. The long-range goal of the course . . . [was] to provide information for voters in the November election (Printed matter of an ad hoc group in a professional school).

But generally, there was little coordination and cooperation between groups. One observer described this situation:

When too many leaflets from different departments arrived at the same shopping center, the head of . . . [one department's] leafletting committee spoke angrily about the "competition" from . . . [the other department]. The leafletting operation had quickly become larger than the organization that was trying to coordinate it.

Two groups attempted to provide some campuswide coordination and leadership for the reconstitution. They were the Strike Coordinating Committee (SCC) and the Internal Strike Coordinating Committee (ISCC). The SCC consisted of representatives from most campus departments and many campus groups. These representatives were generally elected or appointed by those attending the departmental mass meetings following the May 6 convocation. There were over 100 representatives, most of whom were graduate students, although some were faculty, staff, nonstudents, or undergraduates.

Members of the SCC tended to be more liberal or radical than their "constituencies." Although many representatives had not been highly involved in campus activism before this time, all were committed to some form of "reconstitution." In effect, the SCC was representative of those students, faculty, and staff who favored "reconstitution." Their change-oriented perspectives were evident in the SCC proposals recommended at the campuswide meeting in Harmon Gym (see Chapter 1), and are also manifested in a statement which appeared in a mimeographed "Departmental Workbook" (called "The Departments Belong to the People"):

> If the University is to devote itself to discussion and action around crucial social issues, the normal operation of departments must be suspended. Departments must begin to function with the active participation of everyone in them, including students, nonacademic employees, faculty, and other members of·the community. . . .
> Crucially important topics that will inevitably emerge from the very fact that we would engage in such discussion are: criteria of academic competence; the relation between students, faculty, staff, and the whole community; undergraduate and graduate curricula.

The SCC had·little legitimacy in the eyes of many faculty members, students, and staff. In composition, the SCC was not "representative" of the members of the university at large. Some faculty, students, and staff saw the reconstitution as an illegitimate activity which was political and not academic. But even many of those in favor of the reconstitution felt that the SCC did not involve a cross section of people in a full discussion of the direction of the reconstitution. The meeting in Harmon Gym was particularly responsible for these feelings. After that meeting, many labeled the SCC "elitist" and "irrelevant," and campuswide unity diminished. Some members of the SCC themselves had ambivalent feelings about the decentralized character of the reconstitution: "It was good for the departments that they did things for themselves, but it was very bad for campus solidarity. . . . On the one hand, people didn't want the SCC to exert leadership, and on the other they wouldn't do it themselves."

Within the SCC, there was some mistrust between moderates and experienced activists. There was a tendency for individuals to stereotype each other. Some said that the "radicals" were using the reconstitution for their own ends, that is, for building a student movement. Others condemned the "moderates" for a lack of political awareness and for their past apathy. Unfortunately, these conflicts did not usually lead to constructive dialog, as this statement by a member of the SCC Steering Committee indicates (32 people served on a Steering Committee to implement the larger group's policies):

> I was very put off by the tendency of many to say, "this is bullshit," if a discussion went more than one-half hour. They were used to doing their own thing and weren't patient enough to talk things out—unwilling to listen to people either more conservative or radical than they. On the other hand, some didn't exert the necessary self-discipline to not repeat what others had already said.

While the SCC was primarily concerned with giving direction to the reconstitution, the Internal Strike Coordinating Committee had the responsibility of coordinating reconstitution activities. The senate of the student government association (ASUC) established ISCC to create a framework which would facilitate communication between campus groups and provide individual students with more opportunities for participating in antiwar activities. For example, many students who had no departmental or group affiliations were able to become involved in the antiwar activities and coordinating operations of the ISCC.

These activities were centered in Eshleman Hall, which houses the student government association and student activities offices. Activities at Eshleman Hall appeared chaotic to many students:

... hundreds of volunteers scurried in all directions over four floors of Eshleman Hall.... Strike workers outlined a complicated chain of command, though the word "command," they emphasized, is antithetical to the entire concept under which this volunteer work is being done. At present there is, at best, a confusing interrelationship among coordinating groups of student strike volunteers.... These people are organized into about fourteen different committees such as leafletting, campus solidarity, labor, media, etc. (*Independent Californian*, May 3, 1970).

Although the leadership and coordination provided by the student government association was poor in many respects, the reconstitution precipitated a more intensive consideration of needed reforms in the association. One student government officer said: "We in the ASUC had talked about change for a long time—the ASUC is not conducive to communication, it's irrelevant ... The reconstitution climate made ASUC senators more receptive to the idea of reconsidering the philosophy and organization of ASUC." And another student official said that "although power struggles, games still exist—there has been a greater sharing of responsibilities."

PEACE BRIGADE One member of the Peace Brigade has said his group is "... a loose construction of people believing in nonviolent action. People are doing many independent activities.... We don't have any dogma or grand underlying philosophy." Another member adds that "[Nonviolence] is not mere abstaining from violence, but 'force of truth,' 'force of love,' and necessity for fundamentally altering human relationships ... [as an alternative to] coercion." The Peace Brigade was formed shortly before the reconstitution. During the anti-ROTC demonstrations in April 1970, the members of the Peace Brigade took strong personal and collective stands against the war, but also against campus violence. At one point, the Peace Brigade positioned themselves between demonstrators and police, helping to defuse a potentially violent situation. An organizer of the Peace Brigade explained the reasons for their actions:

"We are not a haven for reactionary people who are opposed to radicals and radical violence. We are committed to presenting a nonviolent, alternative way of seeking solutions to the same issues."

Through their activities in April, the Peace Brigade had an important effect on the reconstitution. Many students agreed: "That the Peace Brigade preceded the Cambodian crisis *did* have an effect. Since people were disgusted with violence . . . and had a feeling of powerlessness, Peace Brigade set a good tone for the strike" (From student interviewee). The Peace Brigade showed that effective nonviolent protests can be made, and that strong social protest is the most constructive alternative to violence and suppression. They gave many students hope that constructive change was possible. Moreover, their actions convinced a number of moderate students that social protest is legitimate and necessary. They emphasized that each person must improve the society through his own actions. Their strategy of social change can be described as "cultural" rather than "political" revolution (also see Chapter 4):

Tearing down the structures isn't enough. A government takeover—either through political process, through violence, or through nonviolent civil disobedience, would only put new faces in the same old roles. We are trying to build new roles—or to go beyond the roles to a higher reality.

All of this includes not simply working for change, building the strength of a movement that will one day prevail . . . it means living the "post-revolutionary life-style" now. It means living in a framework in which the ends never justify the means, in which we don't hurt ourselves in the hope that it will build a better tomorrow.

I think that's one of my major reasons for becoming involved in non-violence as a philosophy and as a political activity. It is a frightening thing to see youg people fighting the establishment with its own tools, and thus becoming corrupt, destroying their own integrity in the process (*Gentle Strength*, June 13, 1970).

During the reconstitution, the Peace Brigade tried to help people think of concrete ways they could participate in nonviolent social change:

If you pay U.S. taxes, then YOU PAID FOR THE BULLETS USED AT SONG MY AND KENT STATE. Why not join the many citizens who refuse to pay U.S. income and excise taxes? Why not refuse to pay for the massacre of Vietnamese and the murder of Black Panthers? Why not refuse to pay for death and oppression? (*Ibid.*).

At the May 6 convocation, the Peace Brigade collected over 1,000 draft cards. Their message was:

Action that affects "Middle America" may be the only thing capable of ending the War. That is, the risk that you take and how well you communicate your sense of commitment may be *the only thing* that will move your relatives and friends. By following up the act of turning in your draft card as suggested, your *one* act can multiply itself *dozens* of times (Peace Brigade leaflet).

During the summer, some members of the Peace Brigade started a political commune (as did some other groups). They expressed concern with the limited effectiveness of demonstrations, and said that new forms of collective action were needed:

Our demonstrations have mobilized many people and created some results, but we certainly cannot glorify the outcome, since the war continues. Because of our actions, most Americans are now for "peace," believing that we should get out of Vietnam. Even President Nixon must now carefully couch his actions in "peace language". . . . But behind his rhetoric the war continues.

We should know by now that Nixon will not end this war. And we should realize that the finnicky men in Congress will do nothing (as the defeat of the McGovern-Hatfield Amendment once again proved). We have also seen what once-a-month star studded peace rallies will do: bore us.

We much realize that this war, as any war, continues because we support it . . . This means that we can no longer pay for the war through the 10% phone tax or income tax. No longer can we build the bullets and bombs by working in defense plants. And no more can we provide men to fight by cooperating with the Selective Service System.

. . . It is hypocritical to continue once a month protests while supporting the war in our daily lives.

IF WE ALL step together we will be most effective. By supporting each other, resisting will also be easier. Ultimately though, the decision is up to you, for we must each accept the consequences of our actions (*Peace Brigade* leaflet).

STUDENT
RESIDENCES

During the week of May 6, about 25 percent of the students living in dormitories spent most of their time in reconstitution activities and another 50 percent were involved somewhat. The extent of student involvement varied considerably between individual dormitories—from fewer than one-quarter to more than three-quarters of the residents. Projects initiated in the dormitories tended to be on a small scale and usually consisted of petitioning, letter-writing, or poster-making. Most dormitory residents participated in the canvassing activities of various academic departments and the activities in Eshleman Hall. As the novelty of the reconstitution wore off, the minimally involved students dropped out and the more active students reduced their commitment from full-time to two or three hours per day. One-half to one-third took "vacations" from their regular courses and the reconstitution for at least a few days during May.

Residents of dormitories were not usually encouraged by their neighbors to become involved. Students were not questioned if they didn't want to participate in antiwar activities. One student said: "In the dorm, it's 'do your own thing'—no one really helps or hinders you regarding your degree of involvement." Peer groups in the dorm helped students to participate if they were interested in reconstitution activity but didn't know how to become involved. These students felt that they might not have been active in the reconstitution if they had lived in apartments. One said: "You tend to be swept up in the action because there are so many people around you who have information on what you can do. In an apartment, you are more isolated." In contrast, students who had been politically active in the past said they would have participated in the reconstitution, regardless of their place of residence.

Compared to students in academic departments and various special interest groups, students in dormitories have little in common. Their interests, values, and college experiences are quite varied. For most students, their dormitory is a place to sleep and eat, and perhaps make a few friends. It was very difficult for students to organize antiwar activities in such an environment. It is noteworthy that one of the most active dorms was the home of the Residence Program—a "living-and-learning" experience where students share the same curriculum. These residents tended to be a little more to the left politically than students in other dorms, and they knew each other better. One student believed: "It was very convenient to have people who knew each other working together."

The residence halls staff acted to prevent the little substantial collective political activity in the dorms during the reconstitution. In the dorm mentioned above, the head resident refused to allow the dorm governing body to use its social funds for political action, and outside groups were banned from using hall facilities. When another dorm became the center of activity for a student government group, the Nonviolent Action Party, and for the dormitories in general, the housing administration stopped this activity. The administration objected to participation by students from outside the dorm.

There was more reconstitution activity in student-run cooperatives than in the dorms. One student commented: "Co-ops seem to be really active—more than the dorms. Maybe it's because they are more organized in living together because of the work organization which is involved in their living group." The upkeep and management of co-ops is the responsibility of the residents; the residents participate in small work units throughout the year. The shared work relationship and the responsibility for their living environment tend to foster a greater sense of community. This, along with the fact that these students tend to be more political, resulted in the initiation of reconstitution activities, such as canvassing, in the co-ops.

Students in fraternities and sororities were only about as active as dormitory residents. Initially, less than one-fifth of fraternity and sorority residents were active in the reconstitution, although in a couple of houses, more than half were spending much of their time in the reconstitution. In a few houses, the majority of the members were neutral or opposed to the reconstitution. One very active sorority housed a speaker's bureau and political science courses, and for awhile, the house served as a center for leaflet distribution and child care (*Gentle Strength*, June 13, 1970).

In general, students did not participate in the reconstitution through their place of residence. The factors which seemed to facilitate the organization of reconstitution activities in some residences were a sense of community among residents and the presence of more than a few students who might be called "activist-prone."

THIRD WORLD STUDENTS AND STAFF

While white students reacted in shock and horror to the Kent State killings, Third World people, who experience oppression and violence as part of their daily ghetto existence, expressed indignation and pessimism that only when whites became the victims of oppression was there a nationwide swell of protest and demonstration. A group of black staff members at a campus research center (who formed a caucus) issued this statement:

The recent events in South-east Asia and the murders at Kent State have dramatized to much of the nation, and to the universities in particular, that collective action is required for the country to alter its movement down the path to militarism. We are in full support of the "redirection" of the university and its activities to the end of averting a military dominance of our foreign policy. *We are equally opposed to military dominance on the domestic scene.* Long before most whites in the United States had come to realize the pathologies of unattended and unscrutinized militarism abroad, Blacks generally understood the problem on the domestic scene as it connected with the central issue of racism. For while we, as Blacks, share in the denunciation of the slaughter at Kent State, we call your attention to the slaughter of Black students at Greensboro, South Carolina, last year, when the only response in the white part of the nation was a soft whisper of "Shame! Shame!"

Chicano students, upon cancelling Cinco de Mayo activities so that an antiwar rally could be held, issued the following statement:

As Chicanos, we know the war machine well. It sought to exterminate us in the Southwestern United States at the turn of the century and now sends our young men to Vietnam where they're killed at a higher rate than any other ethnic group. We no longer have any hope in the ability of the system to work. The exploitation of man by his fellow men is at the basis of the American ways of life and government. . . . Some of us have long recognized that the few who control this country will not give up their power without an all-out fight (*Daily Californian*, May 5, 1970).

On Tuesday May 12, the National Guard killed six blacks in Augusta, Georgia. The *New York Times* reported that at least three of those killed were unarmed bystanders (From *Daily Californian* editorial, May 18, 1970). The following day only 300 people attended a rally on campus to mourn their deaths. Black students in one department wrote:

The Black students are also waiting to see if all the cries of "End Racism" are sincere among the white strikers in . . . [a relatively active department]. Or is it just the same old bullshit of securing the support of Blacks through the tactics of "What affects us, affects you"? Today six Black brothers [were murdered] . . . in Augusta, Georgia, by the racist National Guard there. . . . we have yet to hear any white voices raised in protest of this slaughter; perhaps all the tears and cries of "Murder!" were used up by the Kent tragedy, but the six murdered in Georgia—all black—are just as dead (From the ad hoc group's printed matter).

When two more blacks were killed at Jackson State on May 14, most whites were silent. And blacks became more cynical about the commitment of most white students and faculty to social justice and equality. A graduate student in a professional school made this statement:

. . . The major difference between white liberals and white radicals is the fact that the liberals are not willing to attempt to alter or eliminate those systems which negate the possibility of their visions becoming reality. The white liberal vision is perched on the ever-shifting sands of temporary expediency and makeshift compromise.
    The white liberals who have rushed to the fore of the antiwar movement are not to be trusted. In the final analysis, they are going to do one of two things: they are going to get tired of being morally outraged and allow the movement to die; or they are going to get frightened by the reactionary forces aligned against them and run for cover. Either way, the faithful who are being strung out behind them are going to get screwed. I have seen it happen time and time again.
    Two questions to show where the liberals are:
    How many white liberal instructors now actively involved in the antiwar protests were willing to give full academic credit for antiwar work *before* the administration said it was okay to "reconstitute"?
    How many of the white liberal students now active in the antiwar movement are committed to continuing their "no business as usual" posture until *all* U.S. military forces are withdrawn from Southeast Asia? Before I put my black ass on the line with *any* white protestors *anymore*, I am going to know damn well that they recognize and respect me and my people. The next group of whites I join on a picket

line or charge of the Establishment barricades is going to understand and appreciate the fact that the lives of black-skinned people are just as fucking precious as the lives of pink-skinned people.

My wife wrote a poem last night:

Jackson
and
Augusta
and THEN
Kent

Most Third World students didn't participate in the reconstitution and viewed it as a "white middle-class thing." They often asked: "Where were you [white] guys during the Third World Liberation Front Strike [one year earlier] when we had picket lines." However, many Third World students continued to work to improve conditions in their communities and to end racism. Commenting on what people were doing at the end of the quarter, one black student noted that whites were "still flying to Europe and Tahoe" [taking summer vacations] while blacks were "going home to get things together."

Despite, and perhaps because of, their insensitivity to Augusta and Jackson, many whites became more aware of their own feelings toward other races and of the feelings of some Third World people. In one department, a group of black and white staff members sponsored seminars on racism, using the reconstitution as an opportunity ". . . to increase interracial understanding and everyday working and personal relationships." However, the main result of the reconstitution for Third World students and staff was to further alienate them from white society in general and from whites in the university in particular.

ATHLETES Traditionally, athletes have been among the most apolitical groups on campus. Many felt they had been uninvolved in sociopolitical activity for too long, however, and, during the reconstitution, began to express their political concerns. On Monday, May 11, athletes held a mass meeting that was described in the *Daily Californian* (May 12, 1970):

In a meeting unprecedented in the history of Cal athletics, approximately 150 student-athletes, former athletes, coaches, and other employees of the athletic department met . . . to discuss the national situation and its relationship to sports on the Cal campus.

And when the meeting was over, Cal's varsity football team had voted overwhelmingly not to participate in the remainder of spring practice, the wrestling team had voted to boycott this week's National AAU Greco-Roman Wrestling Championship, and all other teams had voted to protest United States actions in Southeast Asia. . . .

Later in the week, members of the crew team rowed wearing black armbands, and some members of the track team also wore them while competing.

Generally, the coaches argued that athletics should be politically neutral, but one coach told athletes that with "... a decision such as this, let your conscience be your guide" (*Ibid.*). Another coach pressured team members into continuing practice by calling them into his office individually and asking them to explain their reasons for wanting to skip practice.

Several factors seem to have encouraged protests by the athletes. First, many had been enrolled in a student-initiated course, taught by Jack Scott, in which they reexamined their role as athletes, their personal development, and their place in society. Also, these student-athletes had begun to notice that some of their professional counterparts had recently become more active in reforming the society in general, and athletics in particular. Finally, there was a feeling of unity on the campus and many athletes felt a part of the reconstitution; they wanted to reconstitute their activities along with the rest of the university.

NONACADEMIC
STAFF

In many departments and administrative offices, the reconstitution was a time of self-examination and redirection in office functioning and morale. In some cases, suggestions for office reform by members of the secretarial staff were accepted and implemented. In most departments, such as Departments A and B, there were no formal provisions for the protection of staff who wished to participate in antiwar activities. Faculty and students were seldom sensitive to the staff's desire to be involved, and the staff felt separated from the reconstitution effort. Members of the staff often expressed dismay that while faculty and students felt they were building greater mutual respect, these same persons often neglected the needs and concerns of the staff. Sometimes the staff were even excluded from mention on meeting notices and in proposals for departmental reform, even though the Wolin proposal explicitly acknowledged the importance of staff participation. Moreover, students and faculty frequently attempted to facilitate their own antiwar participation by having the staff perform menial chores such as typing and mimeographing. For example, by handing out mimeographed notes, a professor could handle material formerly covered in his lectures so that he and his students could devote more time to peace efforts.

The reconstitution tended to accentuate the extent of staff dissatisfaction with the dehumanizing aspects of their jobs. The following excerpt is from a letter written to the *Daily Californian* (May 12, 1970) by three staff members:

... we are not an integral part of our typewriters; we are human beings with opinions on what is happening on this campus and in this country—and we have the right and the obligation to express them as fully as the faculty and students are doing. . . .

. . . it is hypocritical to say "I am opposed to that war" and not at the same time say "I am opposed to the classification of people and people's rights in the campus community by fabricated differences such as race or sex or titles such as 'faculty,' 'staff,' 'students.'" We are all part of a communal educational process; we should all share equally in all that goes on.

The reconstitution became an important catalyst for many staff members who had long been concerned about the war, racism, and working conditions on campus. Staff concerns proved to be broader than the immediate issues; they included child care, minority hiring, and equal pay for equal work for women.

Some staff members saw this as their first opportunity to discuss mutual interests and dissatisfactions, and to organize themselves for representation in departmental decision making. One staff member defined "real" reconstitution as a community of people with differing skills having equal rights and equal opportunities to be socially involved:

Educative implications [of reconstitution] are far-reaching—that staff are human and on that level they have just as many rights and as much creativity as the academic idol or person they work for. We must break down role patterns before reconstitution can take effect.

In Department C, despite the chairman's reluctance, a small group of staff encouraged him to call a meeting to consider how to improve the staff situation. One staff member said:

This was the first real discussion between staff which wasn't run by the Administrative Assistant. We could relate to one another and exchange ideas and gripes. This is one of the most significant things to come out of the reconstitution.

The staff then planned future meetings at which they could continue to seek improvements in their working conditions, and at which they could make decisions, as staff, to recommend departmental changes. In another department, the staff were allowed to elect a representative who would have a vote at departmental meetings.

To some extent, then, nonacademic staff obtained a greater voice in departmental decision making. But more importantly, they began to organize themselves for future collective actions which might improve their working conditions and provide them with greater opportunities to participate in the educational and governing processes of the university. These efforts are being aided through the continued growth of a strong nonacademic employees' union.

3. Reconstitution: Process or Event?

We noted in Chapter 1 that the Ad Hoc Peace Committee attempted to take a leadership role on the campus in organizing students, faculty, and staff to oppose the war. But more importantly, the Peace Committee worked to keep the campus open for discussion on social and educational issues. The Wolin Proposal and other Peace Committee statements were designed to facilitate interaction among individuals and groups in a process of determining what "reconstitution" would mean. The following excerpt, from a leaflet entitled "What is Reconstitution?" is an excellent statement of the position that reconstitution should be an evolving process:

There seems to be considerable confusion as to what exactly is reconstitution. This is not due merely to people disagreeing, but to the fact that we simply do not know. This should not, however, be taken as a sign of confusion, but rather as a clue to understanding what reconstitution entails.

Behind all of this seeming double talk is the conception that reconstitution is not a mechanical act, such as electing a senior prom chairman, but a political process—in the special sense, roughly, of a community of individuals publicly engaged in the enterprise of determining the management of the events and conditions that affect their lives on the basis of some approximation of a common good.

Reconstitution . . . is an on-going process of indeterminable length. There is no blueprint to be followed. There is no specific set of instructions that must be obeyed. The form and content of reconstitution will have to be worked out by the people who are themselves affected. . . .

To deny the unpredictable, uncertain and therefore creative possibilities of reconstitution is to deny its very purpose—to constitute again the University community. The outcome of this process will be novel. It will call for initiative. The consequences for the future are open.

While reconstitution is not something that can or will be dictated to us by paternal administrators or elitist steering committees, neither is it everybody doing his or her own thing for academic credit. In a sense, the old university was precisely that. The reconstitution process will be a public process judged by public criteria for excellence. Neither undefined masses nor leaders will dictate, but individual actors engaged in public discourse within the context of their particular communities—classrooms, departments, colleges—will decide.

Protest becomes an outmoded concept, for this reconstitution movement is not intent on petitioning any leaders to take action on our behalf. We are no longer protesting someone else's politics. Reconstitution is about making our own politics.

To say that we don't know the precise forms of reconstitution is not to say that we know nothing about it. . . . In the spirit of the Wolin resolution, adopted May 6 at the convocation, there are certain guidelines we have agreed to follow. (1) The purpose of reconstitution is to free the resources of the university to work for activities related to ending the conditions of the war in Southeast Asia. This is a common and public criterion by which reconstitution may be delimited and judged. (2) These activities are now understood to be legitimate academic work. And finally (3) decisions on how to implement the process are to be made not by professors, not by administrators, not by student leaders alone, but by the very people whose lives are involved, acting collectively in their communities.

So although some may have viewed the reconstitution as an event, as only a massive but brief protest against the war, for others it was more than that. It was a time for commitment (or recommitment) to a process of experimentation:

We must call upon our imagination and our humanism to develop new alternatives to education, particularly in the academic departments. A new sense of fellowship and social responsibility must permeate our individual actions, the groups we work with, and the institutions we construct (*Daily Californian* editorial, May 12, 1970).

Was the reconstitution only an event? To what extent, if any, did it become a process? To answer these questions, we must analyze the development of the reconstitution itself. There are several questions relevant to that analysis: Why did the actions and interactions at Berkeley during May 1970 take the forms they did? Why was there so little violence and disruption? Why was collective action, and the departure from normal activity, so massive? Why did many people drop out of reconstitution activities abruptly after a couple of weeks? And particularly, to what extent did members of the university create a process of experimentation *within* their departments and groups? What factors facilitated or impeded the development of that process?

The events often produced an emotional as well as a rational motivation to act. One student said: "What am I doing when this society may not exist and we may not be ourselves physically in a war. [The war] never touched home before, I finally *felt* threat." A faculty member, although opposed to reconstitution, commented: "Outrage at extension of the war and the illegal actions of our government have broken down the usual constraints of our society. Massacres in our own country helped to build up tensions."

However, it was the campuswide convocation on May 6 and the Wolin proposal that provided a basis for continuing discussion and collective action. Many people agreed that the convocation ". . . established a sense of community—it brought everybody together—it was the whole key to what the reconstitution means. Participation in classes, departments, antiwar activities wasn't as a lone, single activity but as a whole" (From student interviewee). The Wolin Proposal encouraged students, faculty, and staff in the various departments and groups to discuss what "reconstitution" would mean to them. It also helped to legitimize campus activities aimed at educational reform and social change. One faculty member noted: "The basis of discussion is extremely important—that's what helped Wolin—he set the basis of discussion by presenting the 'reconstitution' proposal at the convocation."

The Wolin Proposal represented a synthesis of "moderate" and "activist" perspectives. It provided activists with a nonviolent way of working for social and educational change, and it suggested to moderates in general, and to many faculty in particular, a way of keeping the university open while allowing them to participate in antiwar activity. It was more than a compromise, for it was sufficiently ambiguous to allow for several interpretations, and it encouraged disagreement and dialog on its meaning. Instead of resolving conflicts, the Wolin proposal provided members of the university with a basis for experimenting with different courses of action.

The quality of interaction improved, and interaction became more intense during the first couple of weeks of the reconstitution, particularly among those involved in reconstitution activities. Interactions took a variety of forms: discussion of policy in meetings, discussion of strategy in task-oriented groups, and observation of each other's activities. Letter-writing tables, paintings, posters, dramatic skits, graffiti on campus buildings, and large clusters of highly active people were visible signs of common concerns. Visual evidence of unity was important because it reduced the alienation and isolation usually felt. All these forms of sharing experiences provided people with ways to develop commitments to each other while participating in different social and educational reform activities. According to one student: "The atmosphere was one of euphoria—complete release of energies—really bound people together. There was seriousness and political commitment but in a humane sense."

Others indicated that ". . . people were talking more, getting to know each other better." And another student told an interviewer: "I got to know and love people I'd never have been able to know." Moreover, status distinctions became less important as barriers to communication: "Common work tasks and strategy sessions brought people together, often in a cross-class [student, faculty, and staff] format which was very pleasing" (Comment by staff member). The increased interaction and openness meant that while many individuals became closer, conflicts also appeared:

Relationships might have been more strained at first for some, but clarification is a good thing and relationships can now develop more honestly and less superficially (From faculty member).

Climate [in the department] seems better to me because I know more people. Of course, people are more open about their complaints, too, so sometimes it seems worse (From staff member).

The learning process was facilitated by the intensified dialogue and interchange of ideas during the reconstitution. Some felt that they were ". . . successful in gaining and exchanging information, experiences, and feelings." One student, who was uncertain of her position on the war, described her experiences during the reconstitution:

I've been challenged. My boyfriend is against the war, and we've gone around and around. . . . I know somewhat better now where I stand, but not completely. I have read up on the war and so I understand it better now. This is partly a function of the dorm—I can understand the views of others, and my own views have been crystallized. . . . The antiwar people have really been very good. . . . They understand that I'm trying to understand where I'm at. . . . My friends haven't pressured me. . . . And we haven't become any less friends since the start of this.

Too, some students became less sure of their own attitudes even though they generally developed a greater understanding of the issues. One said:

At first I was very antiwar, but I have begun to read magazines and newspapers—I wanted to know what was happening, so I went back to last month's issues . . . But I'm still not sure what I'm against. Now I'm mixed up and I'm neither for or against Nixon.

For a couple of weeks, a number of students, faculty, and staff were cooperatively participating in a process of "experimentation." In contrast to consensus-seeking, individuals engaged in much dialog and some open disagreement, but unlike polarized situations, individuals respected one another. However, after a week or two, few people were still participating in such a process, and the reconstitution became an event, past history. Only a few groups and departments, such as the Peace Brigade and Department C, continued a high level of activity.

Generally, the scale of activity died down when interaction between individuals and groups at the university decreased. This situation can be explained in part by the feeling: "One of the most tentative forms of solidarity between us exists when we want the same thing, but want nothing from each other." (This general principle, suggested by social psychologist R. D. Laing (1967) seems to apply particularly well to the reconstitution.)

The mass meeting in Harmon Gym was partly responsible for limiting campuswide dialog on the definition of reconstitution. The Strike Coordinating Committee's definition was too specific and removed the "constructive ambiguity" from the Wolin Proposal. In effect, the SCC defined the reconstitution as a "radical" movement, and as a result, many people either dropped out of the reconstitution altogether or went their separate ways. One student concluded that, "Things have to be changed by individuals helping individuals rather than by mass movements, because mass movements are coercive." The meeting in Harmon Gym tended to finalize the definition of "reconstitution" and to discourage continuing interaction between individuals in different departments and groups, thereby helping define reconstitution as an event.

In contrast, most departments and groups spent so much time on meetings during the first week of reconstitution that people often became bored with the lack of "substantive" activity and dropped out of the movement. Later, individuals who were involved in antiwar projects often failed to meet to share and evaluate their experiences. Interaction among people was also prevented by a division of labor—some individuals were "coordinators" or "meeting-attenders," while others were involved in action projects, such as canvassing, leafletting, or letter writing. Most of these latter activities were repetitious and highly specialized, and individuals frequently worked on a series of unrelated tasks over a week—letter writing in Sproul Plaza one day and typing in Eshleman Hall the next day. Under these conditions, many people dropped out.

On the other hand, the individual's commitment and satisfaction was enhanced when he could invest his creative energies in one project, but help with a variety of tasks by being involved in its formulation and responsible for its implementation. Moreover, when participating on one project, the individual worked closely with one group of people with whom his experiences were shared. In such cases, individual involvement lasted longer and was more intense. Indeed, in the more active groups and departments, such as Department C, there was continual feedback between meetings and change-oriented activities. A group would plan activities, try them out, and then evaluate what had happened. Interaction was maximized by the constant interplay between ends and means. Participants would consider the policy implications of their actions, and experiment with the implementation of policies determined in meetings.

In most departments and groups, however, dialogue, collective activity, and sense of community soon began to disappear and the hope for creating an ongoing process of experimentation died. The convocation which had been proposed for October 2 was never held and no events since have evoked the outrage that Cambodia and Kent State did. The collective mood has gone from despair to hope and back to despair again.

FAILURE TO INSTITUTIONALIZE "EXPERIMENTATION"
As noted above, the conditions that permitted and encouraged many students, faculty, and staff to participate in a process of experimentation generally lasted only a couple of weeks. Three related patterns of activity, "flexibility," "consensus," and "activist separatism," prevented continuing experimentation in all but a few departments and in the university as a whole. Flexibility was the most pervasive characteristic of the curriculum during the reconstitution (see Chapter 1 and discussion of Department B in Chapter 2).

The emphasis on flexibility was based on views that the reconstitution was a temporary adaptation to a crisis situation. Some faculty, students, and staff felt that there should be temporary educational reform to allow for political activity. One student said: "Reconstitution means the school operates with different goals for the class to integrate work in the class to a relevant goal which a crisis dictates." Most faculty were willing to allow temporary alterations in academic procedures to permit students to work to end the war, so long as the students didn't push for permanent educational changes. One faculty member complained that the ". . . Cambodian issue was used by people whose concern was not certainly with the war, but with the transformation of the university."

The strategy of flexibility revealed the pragmatic approach of the administration and many faculty who wanted to avoid taking explicit stands. This approach averted open confrontations with both those who wished to continue their usual activities and those who supported redirection of the university. Chancellor Heyns later made the following statement to the Regents:

Our best estimate of the situation indicated that there was no chance whatsoever for normal campus routines, in classrooms or elsewhere, to resume [after the four-day close-down called for by Governor Reagan] and that any attempt to decree "business as usual" would be met with massive resistance by students and faculty. Clearly a policy of "no concessions" would provoke large numbers of students to join forces with the militants. . . . The only viable alternative was to adopt a position of flexibility in the conduct of courses. . . . (Heyns, June 18, 1970).

Some members of the University questioned this transitory commitment to relevance. One student wrote:

> So this is what it takes to make a university education relevant? Four students' deaths, an extension of the war to Cambodia, administrators' fears that if they don't keep up with students' educational demands, the university will be blown up! . . .
>
> I cannot help but wonder why these noble professors, who now feel the urgent necessity to make their subject matter and teaching style relevant, did not feel that way one week ago, or one year ago, or four or ten? Did the war begin one week ago? . . .
>
> What will happen next quarter, when he [Chancellor Heyns] takes all the pretty options for professors, and students, away? Will professors, afraid for their titles, their position, their salaries, go back to irrelevant teaching and research? Will students herd into lecture rooms once again, protecting their right to earn a degree, and make that $10,000 a year more? . . . (*Daily Californian*, May 14, 1970).

The strategy of flexibility, then, was at best a commitment to temporary experimentation. Within some academic departments, the reconstitution may have helped to focus attention on educational issues and to increase student and staff participation in decision making. In a few departments, new programs or courses were established. (However, these "experiments" generally have a very low priority among the departments' ongoing activities.) These reforms were implemented without modifying, and often without even questioning, existing activities, priorities, and goals. For example, one science department added a course on the social responsibility of the scientist, instead of infusing all departmental activities with a sense of social responsibility. While these reforms have satisfied a few activists, many will be satisfied with nothing less than a complete reevaluation and reform of university curricula and decisionmaking processes.

During the reconstitution, some students complained that others ". . . were sidetracked with educational reform." They suggested that this diverted energies from antiwar work, and that faculty and administration would not be willing to make the curriculum more socially relevant anyway. These students were convinced that any impetus for change would have to come from outside the university.

In many departments, such as Department B, some students pursued a strategy of activist separatism, organizing a large number of antiwar activities outside the regular curriculum (see Chapter 2). As a result, these activists were isolated from students and faculty who were interested in more moderate reforms. This isolation was encouraged by the emphasis on flexibility and the view that everyone (particularly those who wished to continue with their normal activities) should be allowed to "do his own thing."

Together, the strategies of activist separatism and flexibility tended to minimize dialogue and discourage the development of continuing experimentation within departments. Also, the isolation of activists seems to have fostered mistrust and misunderstandings between activists and nonactivists. When the activists would sometimes present a few proposals for departmental reform, the two groups tended to look at each other as antagonists, and increased polarization was a frequent result. This situation can be contrasted to Department C, where individuals were not so tied to concrete and narrowly defined ends. Instead, they were more trusting of one another and willing to engage in cooperative action and dialogue. They were often more tolerant of the ambiguities inherent in their commitment to a process of interaction and experimentation.

While the strategy of activist separatism *did not directly* challenge existing curricula and governance processes in the university, it did lead to activities which often provided others in the university (and elsewhere) with a *model* of experimentation. Some ad hoc courses demonstrated to faculty what relevant courses might be like, and a few faculty had the opportunity to engage in an evaluation of the learning process with students more than they had before. One member of the staff noted: "Some professors got feedback from students as to how they wanted classes changed. [In the future] there will probably be more and more of that—there will be student suggestions for reading lists and some student participation in class structuring."

Since the reconstitution, some ad hoc student groups (with occasional participation by a few faculty and staff) have continued to meet, with the hope of effecting educational reforms in their department. Several ad hoc departmentally based groups have also maintained their social action programs; some are contacting professional colleagues in the society at large and some are establishing new community involvements. In the history department, a number of students, faculty, and staff continued to hold discussions with off-campus groups through most of the academic year. The discussions focused on the war, but they sometimes branched out to other social issues. And as a result of the reconstitution, the Center for Research and Development in Higher Education has begun to sponsor seminars with Rotary Club members on various issues in higher education.

In the months following the reconstitution, the Regents and the university administration established guidelines and standardized procedures in order to obtain consensus among the members of the university (see Chapter 1). In discussing the reconstitution, Charles Hitch, president of the University of California system, said: "We were caught off guard. . . . the academic community has always depended heavily upon a consensus of understanding about its work. . . . We are now in the difficult situation of seeing the consensus shaken" (*The San Francisco Examiner* and *Chronicle*, September 20, 1970). Chancellor Roger Heyns presented the following rationale for the guidelines in Campus Report (University of California, November 13, 1970):

In the past academic institutions have functioned quite satisfactorily with few written rules of conduct for the faculty and the rules that existed were very general. . . . Today the increasing uncertainties in the values and rules of society have their counterpart within the universities so that broad consensus on faculty conduct is not automatic and so easily attained. . . . For these and other reasons it is incumbent upon the University to clarify what is appropriate conduct for the members of the University community.

Many faculty and students felt that the guidelines suppressed discussion and were intimidating to those who wished to suggest or try out curricular innovations. President Hitch indicated that student and faculty authority to experiment with more socially relevant forms of curricula is limited. He said: "No course is the property of the individual faculty member nor is it the property of the students enrolled in the course at a given time" (*Berkeley Daily Gazette*, September 18, 1970). The guidelines emphasize that "personal political activity" should be kept separate from official university activity. But in commenting on the definition of "political activity," President Hitch added: "There are well-recognized difficulties in interpreting what is political. In today's disturbed social climate, what is political at one time may not be political at another" (*The San Francisco Chronicle*, September 18, 1970). Yet, there has been no extensive discussion among members of the university on the possible meanings of "political," neither in specific cases nor in general.

The strategy of consensus has tended to suppress constructive disagreement. It has stressed stability rather than a collective commitment to a process of experimentation in which rules and programs are more flexibly defined and continually reevaluated. Rigid guidelines may serve to further alienate the more socially concerned students (and there are many of them) not only from the general public but from the university as well. For example, if a crisis similar to May 1970 occurs sometime in the future, students likely will be forced to boycott classes entirely instead of trying to reconstitute them; the "student" will become a "nonstudent." In effect, such hard and fast rules force the socially conscious and dedicated reformer to make a choice between social involvement and the academic curriculum.

Even in Department C, before the guidelines had been formally proposed, many students, faculty, and staff began to abandon the strategy of experimentation. Moderates seemed to be less motivated to work for fundamental and continuing reform when the openness and fluidity of the crisis atmosphere began to disappear. Activists, on the other hand, became frustrated with the decreasing rate of change, and they frequently ceased to work for reform within the university.

CHANGING
PATTERNS
OF HOPE AND
DESPAIR

Before May 1970 many students who had been involved in previous protest movements (such as People's Park in May 1969) were left frustrated and demoralized. An editorial in the *Daily Californian* (April 29, 1970) stated:

During "People's Park" massive numbers of people were mobilized daily, culminating in the Memorial Day march of 30,000 people. However, after this high point many dropped out and political activity diminished until recently. The "drop outs" saw that even though almost the entire community was mobilized we still lost the Park [to the Regents]. Frustrated with feelings of political impotence, their idealism gave way to cynicism and inaction. They failed to see that the struggle against the present society would be long and tedious. The Park, like Vietnam, symptomized the complexity of our problems.

However, what seemed to be apathy was really like the quiet before a storm. When individuals saw that their frustrations and concerns about society were shared with others who were prepared to act, their despair became a renewed hope in the possibility of effective action. On Thursday, May 7, the following editorial appeared in the *Daily Californian*:

Yesterday the university was ours. There was no need for militant marches or rocks. The majority of people in this community finally refused to continue business as usual . . .
The spirit that guided our actions during the building of People's Park has returned. In one day we turned a mud hole into an idyllic park. In one day the sentiment of the campus community has moved from a political malaise to a viable political force. People are meeting everywhere, organizations are forming, newsletters are being turned out . . . However, after the park the spirit and political commitment of the majority disappeared. While there is a lot of momentum and energy on campus this will happen again unless people maintain and expand their activities into next week and more importantly when exams start. We now have the power to implement many of the changes within the university we have long talked about. We must seize the opportunity to explore new methods and ways of learning. Faculty and students must work together to produce new alternatives—a new community.

The collective mood of hope and the massive student commitment to action gave rise to a strong atmosphere of nonviolence. One student said: "'[During] the first week you could feel a sense of 'let's work together and get the job done.' So much was happening it was wonderful. You could also sense that violence had lost its hold."

The reconstitution activities were generated more out of hope, optimism, and collective support than out of impatience, alienation, and frustration, although all of these were experienced by many students and contributed to the formation of the reconstitution movement. Most students expressed a trust in the responsiveness of the government and policy makers, a trust that the Congress would respond if only they could mobilize enough of the population to let Washington know the mood of the country. This is why their energies were directed mainly into writing letters to representatives, congressmen, the president and his appointees, and into petitions which they hoped would graphically illustrate the mass opposition to the war.

But while the climate during the first days of the reconstitution was characterized by a sense of hope and community, failures and frustrations took their toll and resulted in alienation and despair. Many people reported this change in mood:

Initially, the place was electric. Then things began to shift, then things were reestablished. Level of calm went beyond that to a depression—heavy to walk through here [the university] it was so quiet—heavy, significant time, no jokes, no happiness, guitars playing mournful songs to a commitment against the war. Then, disintegration (Student interviewee).

Initial closeness in some quarters has dissipated with the decay of reconstitution. Kind of like the aftermath of a love affair. Having been close there's a new difference to the distance of the post-reconstitution [department] (Staff member).

During the first few days, there was an atmosphere of participatory democracy, but I'm afraid it died out (Staff member).

What's there to report? One thousand people continue to die every week in Southeast Asia while we try to reconstitute. Everything we do seems a futile gesture of frustrated impotence. . . . We are cheered up briefly after we persuaded the board of the California State Nurses Association to include a strongly worded ballot on the war in their next newsletter to be sent out to 30,000 nurses—then we realize that 6,000 more people will die before the ballots reach the nurses, and even after they have returned them—what difference will it make? . . . We envision academic gardens. We attend the last throes of the coordinating committee. . . . We become irritable and easily angered at each other—yet experience moments of extreme closeness. We have no future—each day brings no more than the guilt of new deaths to bear upon us (From printed matter of an ad hoc group in a humanities department).

Many students dropped out of reconstitution activities because of the expectation that change would come easily. One student noted:

When people didn't see immediate results, some dropped out. Now we have people with the attitude that "it will take a very long fight to end the war." At first our attitude was one of total exuberance, which cannot be maintained over a long time. We must dig in.

Even one year later some students were saying:

Many ... have been deeply discouraged by the failure of previous student movements (like Reconstitution, the Third World Strike, and People's Park) and have given up hope of restructuring the university. Why? Because people didn't realize at first how long and difficult the struggle would be (*Daily Californian*, May 13, 1971).

But how long will it be before some tangible improvements can be seen? Many people ask this question. One staff member said:

The war continues; I have been involved in antiwar activity for two years—on and off—the war continues—gets worse—I don't really want to seem frustrated and "throwing in the towel," etc., but the war is a symptom as is racism, and talk never cured cancer—symptomatic relief may still be relief, but there's been precious little of that! It's their mess; let them clean it up. I have neither the time, money, power, nor do I know how to use dynamite. I am sick of the idea of being responsible for an "America" I have come to feel is about as worthy of saving as an oil slick. I feel "used." Save America from Reagan and Wallace and Nixon; give it back to Rockefeller and the Kennedys; the Duponts and I.B.M. They did such a groovy job with it when they had it. Let ALCOA clean up its own mess; I don't want to collect aluminum beer cans.

But in some cases, hope persisted. When individuals were part of a community engaged in a process of experimentation, they kept their hope. When they could see someone else trying to deal with the same problems they were concerned with, when they could talk with others about their failures and successes and then formulate new plans of action, they remained hopeful. A faculty activist said:

I do feel that there has been considerable growth resulting from reconstitution. People have come together and shared their feelings and frustrations. The level of alienation within the university is less awesomely large and cold. People were making connections with each other in new and important ways. They will seek out others before acting unilaterally.

In departments and groups such as Department C and the Peace Brigade, where there has been some persisting sense of community, people have been likely to feel that their actions do make a difference even if there have been a lot of failures. A month after the beginning of the reconstitution, when the mood of the campus was despair, a member of the Peace Brigade wrote in a letter to her family:

> But this movement—the movement for a peaceful "revolution," a revolution [that] is at once much less and so very much more than the word typically implies—is very real. It is real enough to trouble the sleep of the president, and to allow faculty of a university to permit incredible restructuring of the academic process. It is real enough to strike chords of fear and yet also chords of timid but growing hope in the hearts of a great many people. It is real enough to have become not only a part but a moving force and a north star in your daughter's incredible, and fascinating and very joyful journey (*Gentle Strength*, June 13, 1970).

VIEWS OF THE UNIVERSITY— AGES OF TODAY, VISIONS OF TOMORROW

The reconstitution at Berkeley raised many questions about the relation of the university to the society. One was: What is the university and what should it be? Such issues were discussed as individuals and groups tried to make decisions about actions to take during this crisis situation. Most of the individuals who favored some form of "reconstitution" did not believe that the university was politically neutral. One student observed that most faculty and students in his department (one of the social sciences):

> ... do not stress political neutrality of the university because they feel the university has never been neutral. The university's involvement in war-related research and ROTC—in the perpetuation of the status quo—have placed the university in a situation which is not neutral but which sides with the government.

One faculty member who was opposed to "reconstitution" expressed the view of many of his colleagues in the university:

> The statement that the university serves the status quo is nearly the opposite of the truth. It seems to me that the university more than any other institution has countered that status quo and has effected the kinds of changes we want. A university in a form much like the present one, rather than one in the hands of a mass populace, is most likely to effect change.

However, some students and faculty questioned the extent to which the university has encouraged social criticism. One student suggested that the views expressed in the university are not as pluralistic as some might think:

> To those of us with neither tunnel vision nor an idolatrous faith in our government, it has long been apparent that there is a working relationship between Wurster Hall [the College of Environmental Design] and

the Pentagon. This is a bond sealed not by defense contracts or even a curriculum in military design and planning, but rather by something much more indelible—a commonality of assumptions about civilization and progress. . . .

. . . The most important function of a reconstituted College of Environmental Design must be to dispel the myths of Western Civilization and debunk the mystifications which inhere to the American sense of environmental progress. . . . (From printed matter of an ad hoc group in a professional school).

The supporters of a nonpolitically involved university often agreed with the activists—up to a point. They agreed that the university has often supported the status quo in the past. One student felt that:

The university should be an academic agency, not a political forum especially for only one side of a political question. Before it was for the establishment side and now it is for the other side—both of these are wrong. . . . The state provides the university as an open forum. This is also one-sided because this is beneficial to the state. The state would also take away open forum privileges to some extent if the university continues antiwar activities. . . .

Those who believed that the university is neutral, or could be neutral, felt that neutrality would be desirable. To these individuals, the university should be a place where one considers theories and ideas, but remains aloof from action. One faculty member elaborated on this point:

The University may be on its way out. The basic strength of the University is as an "ivory tower." An ivory tower where scholarship and training are pursued apart from the rigors of the "real world."

There is a misguided belief within the present mood that the University can become more relevant, more real, more problem-oriented, etc. As soon as the University gets on this track (and it is) it can only lead to its dissolution into the real world. . . .

I enjoy teaching because the University emphasizes theory over action. I enjoy practicing architecture because it emphasizes action over theory.

The reconstitution is a no-man's land between theory and action. . . .

. . . I opt for an either/or situation. . . . This may mean alternating periods of work in the two worlds. Some students may go to work after high school and then enter the University when they feel the need for a more theoretical framework (From printed matter of an ad hoc group in a professional school).

However, another faculty member expressed the opinion that:

In view of a grave threat to democracy from within the government and perpetuation of immoral war, I feel strongly that the values of the University in general, and teaching of . . . a social science subject specifically, can best be served by redirecting our efforts toward antiwar and pro-democracy protest activity (Printed statement issued by professor to his students in a social science department).

There were others who believed that the university should generally be as neutral as possible, except during certain crisis situations such as this one. One group issued a statement that, "The University, in this situation, should dedicate itself to a higher goal—to serving the welfare of the community of which it is a part rather than to maintaining academic routine" (From the printed matter of an ad hoc group in a humanities department).

Others believed that the university is not neutral and must begin to play an actively humanizing role in the society:

This society will not survive with minor revisions and amendments. Problems of crime, poverty, environment, hunger, racism, housing, education, militarism, imperialism, drug addiction, alienation, ad nauseum appear to grow more insoluble with each passing year. . . .
. . . Education can no longer remain a silent partner to this madness. . . . Until the "educational" institutions of this country break out of the shackles of the military-industrial complex there will be no education, only the present training and indoctrination. . . . (From printed matter of an ad hoc group in a professional school).

Students also differed in their views about the relevance of university education to their lives. One student wrote "[the] . . . Strike is misguided. Students should continue with their classes, learn to discern truth from falsehood, learn to think and reason for themselves, then go out into world and correct evils of *world* society responsibly" (From questionnaire completed by student in ASUC poll). But another asked:

What good will . . . [a college] degree do if the kind of society which you have to live in is repressive? There is a very good chance that this will be the last large nonviolent effort to effect social change in this country. After this comes violence and then severe repression (From printed matter of an ad hoc group in a professional school).

4. Lessons from the Reconstitution: New Directions and Strategies for Change

Many students, faculty, and staff felt during the reconstitution that opportunities for learning, individual growth, and cooperative action were far greater than usual in the university. A faculty member wrote in a departmental newsletter:

I think they [the students] are putting their talents and abilities to very good use. It is a great educational opportunity to be involved here and now in this time, in this place. I just deplore the fact that this fantastic educational experience hasn't always been available to the students.

And one student commented: "In five years, I never worked so hard or exclusively [on an activity] or learned so much."

Many people also felt a greater sense of community. One faculty member noted: "Those students who felt a malaise with academic work felt a greater sense of community as a result of the reconstitution. There was previously no institution whereby students could come together."

Is there anything to be drawn from these experiences of intensified learning and community beyond the reconstitution? In my opinion, these characteristics of the reconstitution—a greater conduciveness to learning and a heightened sense of community—are important because they suggest a new direction for higher education. In this chapter, I will present some implications of the reconstitution for developing strategies that may help us begin to move in that direction.

A DIRECTION: CENTERS AND MODELS OF EXPERIMENTATION
The primary purpose of colleges and universities should be to extend to students, faculty, and staff—and to all individuals and groups in the society at large—the opportunity to come together and experiment with alternative ways of thinking and acting. Colleges and universities should help people develop the ability to formulate new alternatives and to continually reexamine existing situations. Indeed, the university did this to a greater extent than usual during the reconstitution. Students, faculty, and staff often reevaluated their habitual patterns of thought

157

and action, and also encouraged individuals in the society at large to think about the war, national priorities, and their social responsibilities. Moreover, reconstitution activities were aimed at making other institutions in the society more "open"—that is, more supportive of an examination of new social priorities, new personal responsibilities, and better ways of achieving traditional ideals (e.g., democracy and objectivity). In particular, many professions were affected, for professionals in the society at large were encouraged by students and faculty to become more socially aware and more prepared to act in light of their social responsibilities.

Activities in this direction give distinctiveness to the purpose of higher education among society's institutions; however, they also recognize higher education's important interdependence with those institutions. Higher education should lead other institutions, groups, and individuals in formulating and experimenting with new alternatives. Hopefully, other institutions will be informed by higher education's experimentation with new forms of living and will undertake further experimentation and ongoing evaluation of their unique institutional activities. The purpose of higher education is to stimulate and initiate such experimentation and to provide a model for developing regenerative processes of "thinking-and-acting."

Toward a
Socially
Responsible
University

Some of the activities during the reconstitution suggest, in concrete terms, what such a university might be like. In particular, many reconstitution activities constituted attempts to improve the quality of learning in the university and the society by increasing interaction between members of both sectors. The mobile community seminars, organized by faculty, students, and staff in the history department were a good example. They were explained this way:

> We are encouraging . . . non-university people to *participate* in the off-campus seminars [composed of 5-7 students, faculty, and staff specializing in the history and present status of various social problems], on an equal basis, in groups of 20 to 30. The small seminar is usually considered the most productive educational form within the university; our goal is to expand and *transform* it so that it becomes a new and attractive form of "town-gown" cooperation in political education (not propaganda). . . .
> We are educating ourselves through our contacts with "outsiders," thus complementing the education they receive through us. . . .
> We invite students and faculty from other departments to join us, thus breaking down artificial intellectual barriers.

Another example is provided by students in the arts. Music and drama students performed in the streets, while some art students constructed a mobile art gallery which traveled around the state. One student wrote of this activity (*Daily Californian*, May 13, 1970):

The University of California-Berkeley has become a piece of art. Though its art museum has closed down, its concert halls are empty, its stages are dark, this campus has perhaps for the first time realized the real function and meaning of art: to communicate, to change perceptions, to make us react.

Art, drama, music have taken to the streets: out of their ivory middle-class towers and to the people. All sorts of barriers are being broken down: art history students are silk screening alongside art practice students, journalism activists are working with design majors to make effective leaflets, sculptors are designing sets for drama students' street theatre. We've destroyed the artificial walls, and our energy and creativity are expanding at a rate unfathomable to us just one week ago. Art students here are proving that art does, indeed, have relevancy to social and political change. And at this campus, anyway, we have made social and political change as art, as well.

Members of the community were also invited to attend "open houses" at the university. Some participated in special discussion and sensitivity groups which brought them together with students and faculty to exchange their views and feelings about social issues and each other. One staff member expressed the hope that continuing education and exposure to new ideas and feelings could be provided by the university for people of all ages and walks of life:

Every person in society should be afforded the leisure and opportunity for expanded awareness, discovery of world and self. Blue collar workers should be exposed to a year, six months in a university/encounter environment . . . . summer sessions for mental and emotional growth (paid by company employers) instead of a summer training stint with the Reserves or Guard.

During the reconstitution, increasing numbers of students and faculty expressed their concern that the university is socially irresponsible. They took the position that the university is an integral and necessarily non-neutral part of society with unavoidable social responsibilities. They felt that to be unaware of the social implications of their professional and academic activities is to run the risk of having a destructive effect on the society—or, at least, of failing to play a constructive role at a time when there are so many problems to be solved. Furthermore, many suggested that the current curriculum supports those in positions of power in the society. For example, the ROTC program trains officers to fight in Vietnam, but there is no department with the goal of preparing students for effective participation in a movement for world peace. In general, one of the most important implications of the reconstitution was that many students and faculty began to recognize their social responsibilities as academicians or professionals and to experiment with ways of improving the society through professional and academic activities.

Even traditionally inactive engineering students began to consider their social responsibilities as engineers. Many members of the department agreed that ". . . engineers are beginning to think politically," and in the future ". . . will be a lot more concerned with politics." A number of engineering students and a few faculty contacted engineers in the society during reconstitution to discuss their social responsibilities. One of their leaflets read in part:

In the past few days, a thousand Engineering students at Berkeley have redirected their usual daily activities to the cause of ending the war in Vietnam. . . . Because of this concerted effort, Engineering students have been recognized for the first time as a socially responsible force. We can no longer afford to allow the stereotypes of us as socially irresponsible technicians to be sustained. To do so, in light of the events of recent days, would be damaging to the cause of peace—both on this campus and in Southeast Asia. . . . We of the Engineering College have the opportunity to alter favorably the character of dissent, not only in Berkeley, but in the Nation.

A number of courses were reconstituted to make them more socially relevant. This was particularly evident in the social sciences and the socially oriented professions, where research could be directly applied to social problems. But in one physical science department, some students proposed a course on ". . . scientific matters which are of special relevance to society" (From printed matter of ad hoc group). And students in some language classes translated political statements of general relevance to United States foreign policy from the newspapers and broadcasts of other countries.

Many other changes in the official activities of the university reflected increased social concern. For example, the staff of the Engineering Library reported (From printed matter of ad hoc group):

The staff has organized a Social Awareness Collection as an ongoing project. The theme of the new collection is "The Social Responsibility of Engineers in a Peace-Oriented Society." Approximately seventy books have been collected to date, on subjects ranging from the war and chemical and biological warfare to the environment and the social effects of technology. All the books in the collection have been donated or purchased from donations. All are available to borrowers for overnight use. The staff has formed a permanent body, the Engineering Library Redirection Committee, to coordinate the new collection and to formulate further plans for a redirection of the library.

Also, some departments held their own graduation ceremonies, which were more socially relevant than the usual campuswide ceremony. Changes aimed at increasing social relevance were particularly apparent in the College of Environmental Design's ceremony:

> Innovations for this year include: cap and gowns optional, a loan fund established by the graduates within CED for minority students, exhibits which display not only student classwork but also professional work from the public agencies concerned with environmental design (primarily in the urban context) and the "reconstitution" activity in CED from recent weeks, a ceremony which addresses itself to the nature of the times, and social hour afterwards with entertainment by a rock band (From printed matter of an ad hoc group).

Many of the faculty and students who participated in academic activities aimed at social change were very impressed with the quality— even in traditional terms. They found that thought and action could be successfully integrated, and that the quality of thinking can be improved by considering the implications of thought for action, and by evaluating actions. One administrator commented that by getting "... out into the 'real' world. ... some people went through major personality change ... [they] put [their] philosophy to work."

Through their participation in reconstitution activities, some students and faculty became more committed to the learning process and to research, for they saw it in a new, more relevant light. Sometimes students discovered that their chosen profession *could* help to improve the society. One student said: "For a lot of people this has gotten them into [the profession] for the first time—into [professional] nonclass activities. Students became aware that they can use their professional skills for political action." Reconstitution also encouraged students and faculty to reevaluate the curriculum for its relevance in preparing socially responsible professionals.

Toward Socially Responsible Professions There is a new view emerging quite strongly among students of the professions which promises to change the traditional professional code. Historically, professionals have defined their obligations with reference to the client. But there is a growing realization that this has tended to perpetuate the values of those who have the most power in the society. These values are seen by many students and younger professionals as often counter to greater societal and world needs. These professionals are developing a higher sense of human commitment and obligation. For example, a student in architecture said that the professional curriculum should encourage thinking which questions the status quo:

> We need to have situations where those persons who *don't* see the

solution to a company's problems by building more buildings can be heard. We should encourage that kind of thinking. Maybe the solution to a problem is not another building but the firing of a president of the company.

Some law students commented that when they enter the legal profession they will "... be more likely to change places and to raise political issues in the law firms." Another student projected that professionals committed to social change will begin to demand that their employers give them time off with pay for community planning and social involvement. Other students were making plans to try to "reconstitute" their professional organizations to make them more responsive to social problems.

The reconstitution revealed that many professional students see their role as professionals as "participant reformers" rather than as "expert manipulators."[1] Students often expressed considerable concern in their reconstitution activities for helping members of the community at large to determine their own futures. These students view the professional as a resource person and as a facilitator. His job is not to tell people what to do, but to help them become aware of alternatives and provide them with the information and assistance necessary to achieve their chosen alternative. He is their partner in a process of learning and experimentation. Faculty and students involved in the mobile seminars in the history department stated:

Despite the traditional nature of the engagements we are being asked to fill (e.g., panels, debates, etc.), we will make every effort to make them two-way exchanges. We are not interested in sending condescending intellectuals out to "lecture" to the community. We want to disseminate information and promote discussion, not assault people with our supposed expertise.

Toward an Experimenting Community

The reconstitution suggested that if the university is to become a center and model for experimentation, its members must develop new relationships with one another. One ad hoc group of activist students wrote:

Reconstituting the University means nothing without changing the relationships in our own lives. These relationships extend into our work and into our politics, as well as in our homes. The most typical form of relationship in American society is that of boss-worker (master-slave).

Part of working to end the war is changing the hierarchical roles which make university complicity with the war machine possible. . . . Our submission as subordinates makes us as responsible as the decision-

[1] For a discussion of this issue, see Berube & Gittell, 1970, pp. 5-9. Also see, in the same issue, Dumont, pp. 26-31.

makers for the policies which support the war ("I was just following orders") unless we, like those who refuse the draft, say "NO!"

In essence, changes in the university's relationship with the larger society led to changes in relationships within the university (and changes in internal relationships facilitated greater interaction with the society). The war and other problems of our society transcend disciplinary barriers, and more than is usually the case, students and faculty in different departments began to talk about the ways in which the perspectives of their disciplines could complement each other in understanding and acting to solve these problems. One interviewer noted:

The area which has most definitely been affected by the activities in the past weeks is that of interpersonal relations. There has been a decrease in competitive feelings and more of a cooperative feeling among individuals. Of course, this is due to the fact that students are united in an effort which transcends the classroom, grades, and degrees.

Students, faculty, and staff often developed closer relationships with one another as a result of having worked together on reconstitution activities. When people broke out of their everyday routines, they tended to develop more personal, and less stereotyped, relationships with one another.

During the reconstitution, students frequently became more involved in creating and trying out new ways of learning. One student believed that the courses which students initiated or helped faculty to reconstitute ". . . raised the level of factual information that students have and was a great experience for students in organizing and putting together [curricular] programs." He added that, as a result, ". . . [the university has] lost some of its rigidity. Learning that goes on now is not forced or done under compulsion, hence it is more likely to be retained."

To be sure, innovations and increased student participation did not come without difficulties, and conflict and disorganization were often an integral part of experimentation. One student said:

Suddenly friendly classes became huge arguments and battles—even discussing what to discuss became a political issue. The old style of allowing the teacher to have authority over what is discussed meant that discussions were organized. The equality of students and professors in many classes caused utter chaos. I feel that my education this quarter was a waste—I would like to learn about more than just Vietnam. But it *was* good to break out of the lecture structure of classes to discussion groups where there was an open attitude. What I really hope results from the reconstitution is a close relationship between students and teachers.

Moreover, participation in reconstitution activities enabled some individuals to develop better feelings about themselves. One staff member commented: "I feel like a more responsible, worthwhile human being." Quite commonly, students said they felt more competent to effect social and educational change and to play an·active role in the conduct of their lives. One person noted: "Reconstitution made people feel they can do something—that they're part of a larger thing and that they've made a contribution."

Some people were involved in political action for the first time in their lives. One student working at the Strike Coordinating Center slept there and only went back to her dormitory to shower and eat. She said: "For once I have found something meaningful to do. I feel fulfilled and that I've found myself by doing something legal and democratic."

In general, learning and individual development were encouraged by "communal" situations where individual expression and cooperative action enhanced each other. During the reconstitution, Department C and the Peace Brigade were more like communities than most groups and departments. In both, the main concern was with the quality of individual and collective participation rather than with the end product alone. People's attention and energies were focused on "doing," and when conditions surrounding the process were optimal for individual participation and creativity, the quality of group activity (e.g., contribution to the antiwar effort) was also enhanced. In these situations, individuals integrated "work" and "play," and their "personal" and "political" concerns (in effect, individuals integrated their "means" and their "ends").

These groups deemphasized role distinctions and divisions of labor, and group activity was based on the mutual commitments among people and their ongoing interaction in redefining and evaluating their mutual responsibilities (see Chapter 3). For example, some members of Department C wrote:

Our common concerns must be stronger than the differences in our roles. The distinctions prevent real communication and therefore prevent meaningful or long-range cooperative action. We do not suggest that there can be complete harmony in so large and diverse a group— democracy implies a pluralistic society with mutual toleration for differing opinions. By educating many people to . . . [departmentally-related] issues, the involvement of more people can be solicited into decision-making, solution-oriented processes (From printed matter of an ad hoc group).

A look at Department C and the Peace Brigade, in relation to other departments and groups, suggests that communities are based on trust and a common commitment to a process of experimentation, and that rules are continually reevaluated. In such a community, consensus is sometimes achieved, but it is not the end or the goal of the group. When consensus becomes an end in itself, constructive criticism and conflict are often suppressed and new alternatives are ignored or never thought of. A faculty member in Department A said it is ". . . not clear how decisions are made, anyway; there are no votes, and the chairman strives to gain consensus without really meaningful resolution of conflicts." Communities are not aggregates of individuals who believe they can "do their own thing" without affecting others; nor are they closed enclaves. Instead, individuals in communities acknowledge their mutual interdependence, and openly interact, sometimes in conflict, but even then with mutual respect; and they are open to their "external" environment. They respond to the changing context while acting to change it.

Communities are based on a mutual commitment to a process of experimentation, which transcends (but does not negate) each individual's specific ideas about social and educational change. Such a commitment requires a great deal of trust and tolerance for ambiguity among group members. For in a community rules and agreements are ever-changing and disagreements are essential. Commitment to a process of experimentation takes time—time spent discussing differences and learning to live with temporary and continually changing resolutions of those differences. A faculty member in Department B said: "I'm not so sure about community. My time is not unlimited, too much time is wasted in committee."

Favoring "community" over "consensus," one student commented: "I'm not interested in [the traditional view of] democracy—it's a numbers game—I am interested in people doing what they think is right—in taking a stand. Students should participate more." Where trust and collective commitment to a process of experimentation did not exist, individual expression and participation were usually precluded by the creation (or maintenance) of standardized, rigid procedures.

This latter situation was characteristic of many departments, such as Department B, and some student movement groups (e.g., the Strike Coordinating Committee). In these groups, "moderates" (and more traditional students and faculty) and "activists" often acted on the assumption that their interests were necessarily at odds; one "side" could unify only by being polarized from the "other" side.

Toward Ongoing Experimentation
The most significant aspect of the reconstitution was that the crisis atmosphere encouraged people to reconsider their usual ways of thinking and acting. Faculty members began to evaluate their justifications for conducting business as usual, not only during this time of crisis but also during more "normal" times. Students sometimes questioned their reasons for being in the university. And in some cases, students, faculty,

and staff reexamined their life goals. At the least, most members of the university assessed their attitudes about the war and national politics. Many also performed a public service by encouraging some members of the larger society to critically evaluate their own social and political views.

The experimentation and evaluation which was stimulated by the crisis during May 1970 suggests a way in which the institutions of higher education can become, at once, more "socially responsible" and more "objective." I maintain that objectivity and social responsibility can be viewed as aspects of the process of experimentation. Such a process involves considering and experimenting with alternative ways of trying to understand and act in the world. This process is collective as well as individual; each individual continually reevaluates his ways of thinking and acting, and helps others do the same.

When people have their everyday routines and expectations upset, as often happens during times of social and personal crisis, they frequently are initially prone to view their actions and the actions of others as "irrational," "politically biased," "subjective," and the like. I suggest that this is because people tend to think of their everyday lives and situations as representing the "objective" world.[2] However, after reflecting on an unusual situation, such as the reconstitution, people may come to the conclusion that their previous ways of thinking and acting were limited, and that there are other possibilities they had not considered. One student suggested that, ideally, ". . . reconstitution would be a breakdown of [existing] structure, of the categories in people's heads, to a simple structure which allows for more complicated thinking and action." Indeed, an important lesson from the reconstitution was that both reason and emotion are necessary to an ongoing process of experimentation, to working toward greater objectivity and social responsibility. The emotions evoked by Cambodia and Kent State led people to experiment and to consider new ways of looking at the university and the society.

But how can such a process of experimentation be created without the impetus provided by crisis situations? How can people be encouraged to continually reevaluate their lives and the world they live in (a question just as important for physicists and artists as for social reformers)?[3] How can we reconstitute colleges and universities as centers and models of experimentation? These questions are basic to the continuing education of individuals and for greater humanizing of the society.

[2] For a discussion of this issue, see Berger & Luckmann, 1966.

[3] See, for example, Kuhn, 1962.

STRATEGIES: HOLISM AND INTERACTION

The two basic conditions for becoming more open to new ways of thinking and acting are a holistic perspective and interaction among people. In preceding chapters, I noted that intensive and extensive interaction was important to creating a process of experimentation. A holistic perspective, or the ability to see interrelationships among aspects of the world, was also important. During the reconstitution, most of those individuals who attempted to create a process of experimentation saw the interdependence between the university, the society, and their individual lives. One student said:

> What I really want now is to work on reconstituting the United States, the university, and myself. I want to close the gap in my own mind between my own predetermined professional goals and working for the strike. . . . After the war is over, architecture will still exist. I want to determine policies within the structure of the college and society in order to create a vehicle for the movement in the future.

Moreover, the findings noted in this and preceding chapters suggest that holism and interaction seemed to support each other. When individuals had a high tolerance for ambiguity (an aspect of holism) they were more likely to trust others, engage in dialog, and participate in an ambiguous and difficult to define process of experimentation. And, interaction sometimes helped individuals to develop a holistic perspective. On the other hand, when individuals were mistrusting of others and intolerant of the ambiguities involved in experimentation, or when they did not see the relationships between their own actions and those of others, interaction was minimized, and this further reinforced mistrust, lack of interaction, and a non-holistic perspective.

Rigid distinctions between interrelated aspects of individual and collective experiences impeded interaction, and in the absence of intensive interaction, such distinctions flourished. This situation suggests that we are in a kind of "double-bind," for the conditions which could best help us to become more holistic and highly interactive are holism and interaction. But one possible method of breaking out of the double-bind is to become more aware of the tendency to compartmentalize aspects of the world. In considering the situation at Berkeley during May 1970, I have noted that people often made unnecessarily rigid distinctions between the university and the society (or the "real" world), between "personal" and "institutional" or "professional" activities, between "political" and "nonpolitical" activities, between theory and action, between the roles of students, faculty, staff, and administrators, among departments and disciplines, and within divisions of labor in action groups.

My examination of the activities during the reconstitution suggests that two aspects of the university have been particularly responsible for the creation and perpetuation of such rigid distinctions: the certification system and the traditional idea of "academic freedom."

In many ways, the behavior of students and faculty during May 1970 revealed that certification activities, such as grading and the awarding of degrees, are important to the stability of the existing university. When the administration and the faculty wanted to make the university more flexible, they temporarily modified the requirements for grading and awarding credit. Indeed I would suggest that one of the primary functions of American higher education is to certify students for entrance into a vocation or profession, that the main emphasis of the curriculum is not on the learning process but on determining whether the student has fulfilled some standardized requirements for vocational certification.[4]

During the reconstitution, many students found themselves in a position where their vocational concerns came into direct conflict with their desire to participate in reconstitution activities. Those students who saw college primarily in terms of vocational preparation and certification tended to choose continuing with their normal academic work. Other students chose to become politically involved, even at the risk of low grades. Most students, however, took a middle course: they participated in some reconstitution activities but did enough course work to pass, in line with the flexible requirements adopted by most faculty. The stance of institutional flexibility permitted many marginally committed students to become temporarily involved in the antiwar movement.

Unfortunately, under normal circumstances, certification requirements are standardized and inflexible. Since many economic and status rewards in the society are based on the achievement of college degrees and grades, rigid certification procedures often discourage student participation in activities relevant to their social concerns. Moreover, these procedures assume that grades are signs of the quality of learning and that faculty are the experts who are competent to pass judgment. Challenges to the certification system were, in effect, challenges to faculty authority. One student expressed the belief that: "If we abolished all grades now, I bet half of the faculty here would have to leave because they couldn't stand that lack of control." And a student who was involved in proposing changes in Department C commented: "There is a shifting of prerogative away from faculty-designed education and toward sharing prerogative between faculty and students. We must recognize the legitimacy of student-initiated action."

Indeed, certification procedures have tended to perpetuate and rein-

---

[4]For a discussion of this issue, see Bilorusky, 1970; and Becker et al., 1968.

force student passivity, while minimizing active student participation in a cooperative process of learning. For example, one student said:

Classes are being held, but the grade requirements are not as strict. This makes you lose incentive. I was basically through with my classes in terms of papers, so I haven't been going very much to class. I feel that I should be going to class, but I need the push of grades to make me go. A lot of people can learn, but they need grades to keep them working.

Furthermore, many students were more concerned with the competitive aspects of the curriculum than with learning. One student believed that: "Students should have to work hard to get good grades; it should be as hard to get good grades in the social sciences and humanities as it is in the hard sciences." Another student said:

I feel that any instructor would be in the wrong for giving science units for antiwar work, but I do not feel morally wrong for taking these and other units any way I can get them. I'll take the units regardless of whether or not I've learned the material they are supposed to represent. There is no reason *not* to take advantage of the strike so long as everyone else does. I don't like school. I just want the degree so I can make money.

In summary, the university's certification system has reinforced barriers between university and society and discouraged active student participation in the learning and governing processes of the university. The system has helped to prevent the creation of a process of experimentation.

Perspectives and actions based on the traditional ideal of "academic freedom" may well be the greatest obstacles to creating colleges and universities which would be centers and models of experimentation. I suggest that there have been two major problems with the existing definition of academic freedom. First, it is a freedom which has been extended to relatively few individuals (i.e., only to faculty); and secondly, it has emphasized freedom *from* certain kinds of interference rather than freedom *to* participate in certain kinds of activities.

The present view of academic freedom has encouraged thinking which has minimized the importance of dialog and interaction to learning and governing processes. This can be seen in the theme of flexibility and in the tendency for faculty to take a stance of noninterference with respect to each other's professional or academic activities. An interviewer observed that in one department the ". . . chairman said that the faculty could do what they wanted as individuals but that they couldn't force each other to do anything." During the reconstitution, faculty members often invoked the principle of academic freedom to justify the professor's right to conduct classes as he wished, without even considering student views. Academic freedom essentially re-affirmed faculty authority over students.

More importantly, the ideal of academic freedom has defended the faculty member's right to pursue his scholarship without interference from the "outside" world. One activist group suggested that academic freedom has provided a ". . . stable atmosphere for those who do not want to be inconvenienced by the problems of the world, but the blacks and the Vietnamese are inconvenienced every day and for them DEATH IS THE SUPREME INCONVENIENCE" (From printed matter of ad hoc group in a humanities department). While some faculty members suggested that reconstitution activities led to social involve-ment and a violation of the responsibilities of academic freedom, some activists believed that:

> . . . Academic freedom is threatened not *ipso facto* when classes cease to function but when:
> —youthful critics of this nation's policies are treated with scorn and derision by this nation's leaders
> —when this University conducts secret war research in support of U.S. aggression in Southeast Asia
> —when this nation's law enforcement agencies can wantonly murder students on American campuses for expressing dissent (*Ibid.*).

Many faculty feared that reconstitution activities might result in a conservative backlash and a loss of academic freedom. And indeed the actions taken by the Regents during the summer gave some legitimacy to this fear. But in what sense did reconstitution activities violate "academic freedom"? Most activities emphasized working within the system, and there was very little violence. Generally, activities were intellectual; there were relatively few instances of radical sloganeering, most points of view were tolerated, and most activities involved talking to people in the larger society and doing research and thinking on social problems.

Activities were not "academic" in the sense that they were making a difference, particularly in the view of those people in the society who wish to support the status quo. The scale and magnitude of the recon-stitution demonstrated part of the university's enormous potential for stimulating experimentation and change within the society. In the past, whenever the activities within the university have become too contro-versial and too significant in their social impact, powerful and conserva-tive social forces have moved to point out that the university has deviated from the ideals of "academic freedom" and "neutrality." For example, when the Regents barred Eldridge Cleaver and Angela Davis from positions of authority as faculty members, one had to take note not so much of the fact that Cleaver and Davis were saying controversial things but that both of them were successful in influencing many people to become more involved in activities aimed at fundamental social change. (It is noteworthy that neither Cleaver nor Davis used their position as faculty members to engage in what most would call "direct" social action).

The traditional ideal of academic freedom tends to support the status quo by discouraging activities which would lead to substantive change. Because of the incorrect assumption that colleges and universities can be separated from the society and that thought can be separated from action, the ideal of academic freedom has encouraged faculty and student participation in activities which, at best, pose minimal challenges to the status quo. Moreover, conservative forces, such as the Regents, have required that controversial thought be separated from action. Academic freedom has become a freedom which is "academic," for it has been of no consequence, having limited activity to the socially acceptable.

I therefore propose that we begin to formulate a new freedom for colleges and universities, which would indeed be a new freedom for all mankind.[5] For as one group wrote: "Academic freedom is not only a faculty right; it [should be] a student right, indeed, a human right" (From printed matter of an ad hoc group in a professional school). This new freedom should be a freedom to help *humanize* the society, to extend to *all* people *equally* assistance in experimenting with new ways of living. During reconstitution, one student wrote:

When the professor, then, asks about his academic freedom, remind him that freedom can only exist when *both* parties to the teaching-learning relation are free. And ask him to think as well about the freedom of Cambodians, of Chicanos in the Central Valley, and of the men and women held behind bars as political prisoners. . . .

. . . he should fight *with us* to reconstitute the university—class by class, department by department—and to create cooperative social institutions in which the rights and needs of *all* the people are respected (*Daily Californian*, May 12, 1970).

If colleges and universities obtain freedom to become more like centers and models of experimentation, the intensity of their problems will not diminish, but they will be headed in a more moral direction. As faculty, students, staff, and members of the larger society begin to participate in a process of experimentation, they will be acknowledging

[5] I have restricted my analysis in this paper to American society because it is here that the results of the study are directly germane, but I do not believe that we can solve our problems without also considering our relationships with peoples in other countries. However, the strategies through which we might achieve such an objective—which appear even more complex and unclear—are beyond the scope of this paper.

the relation between thinking and acting, and will thereby be improving the quality of the educational process and the conduct of inquiry. In this way colleges and universities might indeed become intellectual communities, helping to humanize the society. Moreover, higher education would be serving the cause of equality by extending equally to all citizens assistance in, and opportunities for, experimentation to improve the quality of their lives.

This freedom will not be easy to achieve nor will it be easy to exercise responsibly. It will be particularly difficult to develop ways to extend equal opportunities for all to participate in the processes of experimentation, and it will be just as difficult to evaluate the extent to which the ideal is being achieved. Moreover, the only society which would be likely to give its full support to such an endeavor is one that has already integrated such a process of experimentation into its own soul. While higher education would be no less neutral than now, its non-neutrality would be more obvious to all, disturbing to most (because of the facilitation of experimentation), and threatening to many people in positions of power. This suggests another double-bind. Higher education and society are interdependent; I do not believe the society can become more open and humane unless higher education begins to stimulate such experimentation. But the extent to which the society will allow higher education to do this depends upon the humaneness of the society.

What can we do? During the reconstitution, two basic strategies were employed by those individuals who saw the need for fundamental social and educational change. One strategy can be called "cultural revolution" and the other "political revolution." Both strategies recognize that the unequal distribution of power in the present society supports a perpetuation of the status quo; however, they differ in their approach to redistributing power and to changing the relationships among individuals in the society. The advocates of political revolution take the position that ways must be found to wrest that power away from the ruling class and to democratically distribute it equally among everyone. This was similar to the views of many members of the Strike Coordinating Committee and activists in Department B.

The advocates of "cultural revolution" argue that if change is approached primarily from the standpoint of power struggles, the strategy will corrupt all those who seek to gain power, even if their struggle is in the name of the masses. Most members of the Peace Brigade, and a number of activists in Department C, took a position similar to this. They suggested that we must reconstitute our lives, individually and collectively, in order to change the society through our own personal conduct.

For example, they pointed out that those in power are supported by our complicity in continuing to participate in everyday activities which support those in power. They suggested that we need new societal alternatives, embodying new values and open to the full participation of all people.

The similarities and differences in these approaches may be demonstrated by considering their application to the mass media. For example, the advocates of both strategies would agree with the following statement which appeared in the leaflet of an ad hoc department group:

The TV news program tries to deny . . . any personal feelings and [purports] that the entire presentation is "objective" reporting. For example, Walter Cronkite is billed as "Mr. Unsensational." A quote on Cronkite's office wall reads: "Viewers rarely recall and relish a Cronkite statement. They believe it instead." [In] another example of TV news furthering the illusion of objectivity, ABC News devotes the last few minutes of their evening news program to "commentary," as if what came before was devoid of any such commentary. From the choices of the news items to the editing of the film reports, TV news is not and cannot be objective, nor is it a machine-like truth teller.

Since television is owned by corporations and since the purpose of the corporation is to maximize profits, all TV programming (news included) must be saleable to advertisers and to the public. When public interests or public service come into conflict with profits, which do you think wins out?

Both perspectives suggest that all social activities are nonneutral and that they usually support the status quo. However, activists, working in an ad hoc group called New People's Media Project, sometimes had different views on the role of the media in effecting social change. One activist proposed a strategy similar to that of "political revolution." According to an interviewer, "he wanted to *use* the power of the media for·radical ends, that is, for radical control of dissemination of information." The interviewer noted that another activist "wanted to lessen the power of the media." This latter strategy, similar to that of "cultural revolution," emphasizes participation of all individuals attempting to alter the character of the media. According to one activist, this involves:

. . . de-mythologizing TV in general so as to increase individual freedom and minimize propagandizing [e.g., get more·local TV, UHF]. If people are more involved in the production of TV then they won't be so awed by it, they'll take it more for granted, be more critical of it, people will have more freedom to choose *which* information to accept, instead of just blindly believing everything they're told.

There are difficulties involved in both approaches to social and educational change. The problem with the strategy of political revolution seems to be that it tends to be self-defeating insofar as power corrupts; with this strategy, the change agent must assume that the ends justify the means, yet this is one of the disastrous assumptions underlying United States involvement in Southeast Asia. On the other hand, the strategy of cultural revolution attempts to integrate means and ends into a unified, ongoing process of change. However, this strategy puts the change agent at a decided disadvantage in the context of a society where most of the power lies in the hands of a minority who are likely to resist fundamental change. The unequal distribution of power in the present society therefore places the change agent in a double-bind. If he is "realistic," his tactics will tend to be self-corrupting; if he is "idealistic" in his approach, he may have greater difficulty in challenging those in positions of power for his methods are based on trust and "fair play." In some sense, both methods are based on self-defeating principles, and their self-defeating character seems to arise out of their relation to the very social inequities they wish to alleviate.

Finally, I must express some preference for the strategy of cultural revolution, for its value consistency and integration of means and ends, and for its emphasis on people helping one another to find better ways of living and learning. During reconstitution, when people became aware of social and educational problems and the difficulties in effecting change, they often expressed feelings of despair and frustration. But when they particiapted in communities committed to a continuing process of experimentation, they began to have hope. While the strategy of political revolution often led to mistrust and polarization (e.g., the meeting in Harmon Gym), and while the strategies of flexibility and consensus supported the status quo, the strategy of cultural revolution sometimes led to trust and interaction, which are necessary to break out of the double-binds and through the barriers which hinder the development of social equality and enlightenment. "Cultural revolution" undoubtedly is slow, but it may be the only way to an experimenting university in an experimenting society.

In this study, I have not been primarily concerned with describing the past, nor predicting the future. I have hoped instead that this study will help us to create the future. We must begin to engage in a cooperative endeavor to experiment with new alternatives, better educational environments. This is not a task which confronts us only in times of crisis and social unrest; it is the never-ending process of creating a more humane and democratic society, it is the process of collective self-determination. This process is described by Hazel Barnes in the Introduction (pp. xxvii-xxviii) to Jean-Paul Sartre, *Search for a Method* (1963):

Sartre states that the ultimate ideal for mankind would be a world in which all men worked together in full consciousness to make their history in common. We occasionally see a first approximation of this in what he calls the "group-in-fusion". . . . In the group-in-fusion there is no longer an I-you division or I-they. Rather it is a collection of "thirds" in which each third is a "myself" inasmuch as all are working to accomplish the same goal. The group achieves ends which are my ends but which I could not attain by myself. The aim of the group is to develop and to utilize those qualities and potentialities which are peculiar to each of its members. At present such groups are generally constituted only in the face of common danger and for the sake of immediate goals . . . But Sartre does not feel this outcome is inevitable. If the common end becomes the liberation of *all* men and if at long last all men join in writing the history of this liberation, then we may truthfully say that there is a single history of man; . . .

During reconstitution at Berkeley, the "commitment" in most departments to a collective process of experimentation was fleeting and short-lived, and in others, it was virtually nonexistent. Nevertheless, the attempts to create such a process gave the situation on the Berkeley campus during May 1970 much of its significance. The flickerings of these efforts are more than "a flash in the pan," as some have said; they are the faint light that can guide us on a never-ending journey that is the reconstituting of our world and our lives. That the journey can never end may give us cause for some despair, but that we can help one another see the source of the light should give us hope. With this in mind, our journey can set us free.

References

Barnes, Hazel E. (trans.), in Jean-Paul Sartre, *Search for a Method*, Alfred A. Knopf, Inc., New York, 1963.

Becker, Howard S., B. Greer, and E. C. Hughes: *Making the Grade: The Academic Side of Life*, John Wiley, New York, 1968.

Berger, Peter L., and Thomas Luckmann: *The Social Construction of Reality: A Treatise in the Sociology of Knowledge*, Anchor Doubleday, 1966.

The Berkeley Daily Gazette, September 18, 1970.

Berube, Maurice R., and Marilyn Gittell: "In Whose Interest is the 'Public Interest'?" *Social Policy*, pp. 5-9 (May-June 1970).

Bilorusky, John A.: *Relevant to Whom?* Paper read at the Western Psychological Association Convention, Los Angeles, April 18, 1970.

Blumer, Herbert: *Symbolic-Interactionism: Perspective and Method*, Prentice-Hall, New York, 1969.

The Daily Californian, April 6, 7, 29; May 1, 4, 5, 7, 8, 11, 12, 13, 14, 15, 18, 21; October 12, 19, 27; 1970.

Dumont, Matthew P.: "The Changing Face of Professionalism," *Social Policy*, pp. 26-31 (May-June 1970).

Gentle Strength, Peace Brigade Newsletter, June 13, 1970.

Heyns, Roger: *Report to Regents' Committee on Educational Policy*, University of California, June 18, 1970.

The Independent Californian, May 3, 10, 1970.

Kuhn, T. S.: *The Structure of Scientific Revolutions*, University of Chicago Press, Chicago, 1962.

Laing, R. D.: *The Politics of Experience*, Ballantine Books, 1967.

The San Francisco Chronicle, September 18, 1970.

The San Francisco Sunday Examiner and Chronicle, September 20, 1970.

University of California: *Campus Report*, vol. 5, no. 4, Berkeley, Calif. (November 13, 1970).

University of California, Academic Senate: *Motion Approved by the Berkeley Division*, May 4, 1970.

Appendix: Questionnaire Facsimile and Total Sample Results

The questionnaire used in the survey of presidents, as well as the results for the total sample of presidents, are presented on the following pages. All the figures are percentages. For most of the questions, two figures are given: the first is the percentage of the total sample (N=1,856); the second, in parentheses, is the percentage of those colleges indicating (on question 8) that Cambodia/Kent/Jackson had had "significant impact" on the functioning of the college (N=1,064). Asterisked figures have been increased by 43 percent, the percentage indicating no impact whatsoever (on question 8). Because of questions not answered (as well as rounding errors), percentages will not total to 100 percent.

July 15, 1970

Dear President:

As we are well aware, various events of this past spring—notably the Cambodia decision and the Kent and Jackson State shootings—have led to a groundswell of feeling and action on the campuses that could have far-reaching consequences for the nature and well-being of higher education in America. The Carnegie Commission on Higher Education was established to conduct studies and make reasoned and timely analyses and recommendations concerning higher education policy in the United States. To better inform our work, we are soliciting through this questionnaire your perspectives on what has happened on your campus in the past three months, and what the future seems likely to hold. Forms have been sent to every college president.

We know that a questionnaire of this sort cannot embrace all the complexities of the situation. A much longer form, however, would be prohibitive for obvious reasons.

We are conscious of the highly sensitive nature of much of this information. Our hope, nonetheless, is to obtain the most accurate data possible, and to this end we wish to respect the privacy of individual respondents and institutions. Please note the option below, of not identifying yourself or your college. For analytic purposes we intend to classify institutions in various ways (by type, region, and so forth) and thus need your answers to the seven questions at the top of the next page.

Since the information to be gathered is most timely, we hope to have a reply from you within a week, if at all possible. A summary of results will be mailed to all colleges as soon as available.

Thank you for your cooperation.

Sincerely,

Richard Peterson,   Clark Kerr
Project Director   Chairman

                               Carnegie Commission
                               on Higher Education

N.B. If the chief campus administrator is away, please pass this questionnaire on to an appropriate, available college official.

OPTIONAL INFORMATION

Your Name_____ Title_____

Institution_____

Carnegie Commission on Higher Education
Questionnaire on the Aftermath of Events in April and May 1970

For each of the questions below, check the *one* alternative that best describes your institution:

Type, level:

Ph.D.-granting university	10%
Comprehensive college I: wide range of liberal arts and professional programs; several kinds of degrees	7
Comprehensive college II: a more limited range of programs and degrees (e.g., strong teacher education)	13
Four-year liberal arts college	26
Professional or other · specialized school (e.g., medical, theological, art, etc.)	8
Two-year college	34
Other	2

Control or affiliation:

Public	49%	Jewish	<1
Independent	20	Protestant	18
Catholic	12	Other	<1

Selectivity:

Freshmen mostly from top 10% of high school class	9%
Mostly from the top 40%	40
Essentially open admissions	50

Level of federal support, 1968-1969:

Top 50 institutions; $14,000,000 or more	3%
Second 50; 6 to 14 million	3
Less than $6,000,000	93

Total enrollment:

Less than 1,000	39%
1,000-5,000	41
5,000-12,000	12
More than 12,000	7

Regional location:

Pacific States (CA, OR, WA)	13%
Mountain States (NV, ID, MT, WY, UT, CO, AR, NM)	4
Northeast (PA, DE, and north)	25
Southeast (AR, KY, WV, MD, and south)	24
Midwest (remaining states)	33

In location, is your campus:

Urban	36%
Suburban	31
Rural	32

Question 8: If the Cambodia decision and the Kent and Jackson State shootings have had no significant impact on operations at your campus, check box #8 to the left and return the questionnaire in the envelope provided. (Please answer questions 1 through 7 above.)

Check any of the following that occurred on your campus during May of 1970.

There was a letter-writing campaign.	29%	(51%)
A campus delegation went to Washington.	20	(35)
One or more groups went to the State Capital.	14	(25)
Anti-war speakers were brought to the campus.	26	(46)
Special seminars, workshops, or research projects were initiated.	37	(65)
Physical facilities on the campus (e.g., rooms) were made available for anti-war or other political activities.	34	(59)

Efforts were made by students to talk or otherwise communicate with people in the local community and region about the war and the campus reaction. 40 (70)

Some students and staff began planning campaign activities in behalf of Congressional peace candidates. 23 (40)

Campus religious groups and leaders assumed a more significant role than in previous months. 15 (26)

Some classes were cancelled. 25 (43)

There was a general student/staff strike or shutdown lasting a day or longer. 14 (24)

There were essentially peaceful demonstrations. 44 (77)

There were demonstrations causing damage to persons or property. 4 (7)

Outside law enforcement forces were brought onto the campus. 4 (7)

Moderate (in their tactics) student-faculty leaders were generally in command of events. 43 (75)

Radical leaders were generally in command of events. 3 (6)

There was resentment on the part of black students and staff about the surge of concern about the war on the part of white students and staff. 9 (16)

At any time did the chief campus administrator publicly take a stand, *as an individual*?

No	31%	(55%)
Of neutrality	5	(8)
In support of the war or the Cambodia decision	<1	(1)
Against the war or the Cambodia decision	18	(31)

At any time did the *institution* as such take a stand publicly?

No	91%	(82%)
Of neutrality.	4	(7)
In support of the war or the Cambodia decision	0	(0)
Against the war or the Cambodia decision	4	(7)

Please describe how this decision was reached:

Faculty vote	2	(3)
All other responses (including faculty participation in a campuswide referendum or convocation)	2	(3)

As a result of Cambodia/Kent/Jackson, were your commencement exercises conducted differently this year?

Yes 7% (13%) No *92 (86)

Did students engage in symbolic (non-disruptive) expressions of anti-war sentiment during commencement exercises?

Yes 17% (30%) No *82 (67)

Were your commencement exercises disrupted in any significant way?

Yes <1% (1%) No *98 (95)

Was protest on your campus:

More violent/disruptive/destructive *after* the Cambodian decision and the Kent and Jackson State shootings?	18%	(32%)
Less violent *after* Cambodia/Kent/Jackson?	2	(3)
No discernible difference	19	(32)
No real protest either before or after	*51	(25)

Approximately what percentage of all undergraduate courses were modified to reflect anti-war interests?

None	*68%	(44%)
Less than 10%	18	(31)
10% to 25%	6	(10)
More than 25%	4	(7)

Approximately what percentage of the faculty modified their final examinations (in either content or method)?

None	*73%	(52%)
Less than 10%	13	(23)
10% to 25%	4	(7)
More than 25%	8	(14)

Approximately what percentage of the faculty modified usual grading procedures?

None	*74% (55%)
Less than 10%	11 (18)
10% to 25%	4 (6)
More than 25%	10 (17)

In roughly what percentage of the departments did secretarial or other nonacademic personnel seek to (or did) modify normal work routines?

None	*93% (87%)
Less than 10%	5 (8)
10% to 25%	<1 (1)
More than 25%	1 (2)

Roughly what percentage of undergraduates went home before the end of the term?

None	*82% (68%)
Less than 10%	11 (18)
10% to 25%	3 (6)
More than 25%	3 (6)

Were the Cambodia/Kent/Jackson events catalysts for active student and staff concern about other issues and problems? If so, please describe.

Issues regarding college functioning:

Three most frequently mentioned themes:

Campus governance, student participation, etc.	9% (15%)
Teaching, curriculum, etc.	4 (7)
ROTC	2 (4)

Issues in national life:

Four most frequently mentioned themes:

Racial injustice	5 (7)
War and peace (in general)	4 (7)
Environmental pollution	3 (5)
Dissent and repression in America	2 (3)

Were there differences between junior and senior faculty in support for involvement in the various activities triggered by Cambodia/Kent/Jackson? Compared to senior (tenured) faculty, were junior (non-tenured) faculty:

Much more supportive	13%
Somewhat more supportive	39
No more or less supportive	38
Less supportive	1

If normal instructional activities shut down for a period during May or June, what was the duration of the cessation?

No shutdown	*79% (62%)
1 day	8 (14)
2 days	7 (12)
3 to 6 days	3 (5)
1 to 2 weeks	1 (1)
For the balance of the term	2 (3)

What were the circumstances of the shutdown? By whose decision or order? What were the sources of pressure to close?

Three most frequently mentioned themes:

Student pressure	12% (28%)
Faculty pressure	7 (16)
Fear of violence	2 (3)

What has been the reaction of particular constituent groups to the various activities of May and June on your campus?

	1	2	3
	Mainly Critical	Mainly Favorable	No discernible reaction
Trustees	10% (17%)	26% (45%)	(30%)
Alumni	12 (20)	16 (29)	(43)
Parents	10 (17)	17 (30)	(44)
Local citizens	17 (30)	16 (28)	(34)
State Legislators	12 (21)	8 (14)	(53)
Local Press	7 (13)	22 (38)	(40)

What proportion of your undergraduate and graduate student body would you estimate is engaging seriously this summer in "within-the-system" partisan political activity (canvassing, leafletting, organizational work, etc.)?

Fewer than 5%	*87% (77%)
5% to 25%	11 (20)
More than 25%	1 (1)

Will there be a recess this fall when students and staff may work in local and Congressional election campaigns?

No	*86% (76%)
Yes; a calendar change (the "Princeton Plan")	2 (4)
Yes; time out from the regular calendar	1 (2)
Possibly; decision not yet made	10 (18)

What would you say has been the net impact of Cambodia/Kent/Jackson on the morale and cohesiveness of your faculty?

Greater division and polarization	14% (24%)
Greater unity	14 (25)
No significant impact	*71 (49)

What would you say has been the net impact on relations between faculty and students?

Greater division and polarization	9% (15%)
Greater unity	23 (40)
No significant impact	*66 (41)

What is your estimate of the general *impact* of Cambodia/Kent/Jackson on *academic standards* (as usually defined) on your campus?

During May and June 1970:

None	*77% (59%)
Detrimental	18 (32)
Positive	4 (6)

During the academic year 1970-71:

None	*81 (66)
Detrimental	9 (15)
Positive	5 (9)

**In which academic divisions were there departures from normal examination and grading procedures during May and June?

	Substantial	Some	Little or No
Business	3% (5%)	3% (6%)	*78% (59%)
Education	3 (6)	5 (10)	*76 (56)
Engineering	2 (3)	2 (4)	*72 (51)
Fine Arts	5 (9)	10 (17)	*73 (52)
Humanities	7 (12)	13 (24)	*71 (49)
Life Sciences	4 (7)	7 (12)	*77 (59)
Physical Sciences	4 (7)	7 (12)	*78 (62)
Social Sciences	7 (12)	14 (25)	*69 (47)
Other			

Do you anticipate difficulty in getting the regular academic program going in the fall?

Considerable	<1% (<1%)
Some	5 (9)
No	*93 (87)
Not applicable; changes are planned.	1 (2)

In your judgment, did the Cambodia/Kent/Jackson events have a positive or beneficial impact on the instructional program on your campus?

Yes	14% (24%)	No	40 (70)

If yes, please elaborate.
Three most frequently mentioned themes:

Greater student/staff concern re curriculum reform	4% (7%)
Greater student/faculty/administration cooperation, communication	4 (6)
Greater student concern about national/international problems	3 (6)

As a result of Cambodia/Kent/Jackson, are there students and/or staff at work this summer, with "official" college approval and/or assistance, planning reforms, or new programs to take effect this fall? If so, please describe.

Planning curricular changes or additions (especially, new courses)	4% (6%)
Other matters—governance, administration, etc.	3 (5)
Work, nature not specified	2 (4)

Are there students and/or staff at work this summer, *without* "official" approval, planning reforms or new programs designed to take effect this fall? Describe.

Some kind of work in progress.	7% (13%)

Have any changes in the academic program *already* been approved for this fall? If so, please describe.

Change of some kind approved.	6% (11%)

Have any changes in campus governance procedures been approved? Describe.

Change of some kind approved.   6% (11%)

What do you consider to be the single *most significant* long-run implications of the events of the spring for your campus?

Three most frequently mentioned themes:

Increased student/staff concern about national/international problems   9% (16%)

Increased student/faculty/administration mutual trust   7   (13)

Violence, alienation from the system, etc.   4   (8)

**Rate of omitting is substantial and varies by division (the latter mainly because some of the divisions, e.g., engineering, do not exist at some of the colleges).